# Crusader Conspiracy

The whole mealtime William sat in silence. A frown crinkled his grandmother's forehead as she observed him. Tom, seated at the lowest table, also watched his charge. As the knights retired to ready themselves for a long ride to St. Pol, the older boy caught his young lord's arm. "Are you sick?" he demanded.

William's eyes were heavy with misery. "I don't know. I want to take the cross so badly I feel sick at my stomach."

Later, Lady Margaret found a moment to corner Tom. "Is what ails the boy what I think it is?"

"He wants to go with the knights on Crusade."

"Always, always! His ambition is always larger than his abilities."

Tom faced her with his quiet, steadfast eyes. "Why should William return to England? Unless he must take the place of Humphrey if that one dies, he must make his own way somewhere. Who knows? It may be in the Holy Land. England is not safe for noble sons just now."

# Crusader Conspiracy

## Lois M. Parker

Review and Herald Publishing Association
Washington, DC 20039-0555
Hagerstown, MD 21740

Copyright © 1983 by
Review and Herald Publishing Association
Printed in U.S.A.

This book was
Edited by Gerald Wheeler
Cover design and illustration: Richard Steadham

**Review and Herald Cataloging Service**

Parker, Lois M.
   Crusader Conspiracy

  I. Title.
     [940.18]

ISBN 0-8280-0166-9

# Chapter One

As William teetered on a twisted branch of an old apple tree, the little falcon, which had escaped him, eyed him coolly from above, then preened a feather.

"Oh, come now, Beauty!" he said. " Hold still just a little. You know it's not safe for you to fly free with the jesses* on your legs. They would tangle in the tree branches, and you would die!"

The bird glanced away, keenly aware of approaching riders whom the boy did not see. He stretched a few more inches and captured the end of a jess. At his pull, the kestrel launched herself, but had to fall, flapping and snapping her beak furiously.

That did it! William lost his footing and tumbled headfirst with a great breaking of leafless twigs. An agonizing jerk at his ankle left him swinging head down, foot trapped in a V of branches.

"Hold still." The voice came from a stocky, dark youth who had watched his plight with an expressionless face but amused eyes. The newcomer could reach William's shoulders, and he stopped his swinging. "Now I will push up so you can free your foot. That's it. Ugh!"

He received the full weight of the 12-year-old William and turned him right side up. The fair Norman boy tested his ankle and made a face.

"It's just scraped a little," he decided. "Beauty is rather cranky about being caught."

---

*jesses: leather thongs

The kestrel ruffled her feathers and smoothed them again, still glaring angrily at the head beside her shoulder perch.

"You should pay more attention and not let her jesses slip through your fingers, if you chose to take her out without a hood. She will have to be restrained."

"Oh, Tom! She likes to see everything, as well as I do—and she sees more than I do!"

Now the horsemen halted beside them. William's blue eyes widened as he looked up at his nobleman father. Tom dropped to a knee in deference to the earl of Hereford, Henry de Bohun, and at the far side of the baron, William's even nobler grandmother, Lady Margaret. William bent in a graceful bow and kissed the hand his father held out.

"In trouble again, son? What would you do without Tom Dobbins to get you out of your scrapes? What was it last time? A millpond bath he rescued you from—in March!"

William managed to look repentant, but the earl seemed hardly to believe it. The boy's attitude changed to eagerness. "If I could have Tom with me all the time, I wouldn't get into so many troubles. He is really sensible!"

His father permitted himself a wintry smile. "And when will you learn to think before you leap? Come."

Without a further word the earl and his royal Scottish mother rode on, their train of followers well behind to give them privacy. The young Bohun trotted over to his pony, which Tom held while he mounted, careful not to dislodge Beauty.

"Come along, Tom. I see my father stopping at your house." The dark boy loped beside the scrambling pony, making easier work of it than the short-legged animal.

"Someday soon," William shouted, "I will have a real horse, and become a knight, and go forth to right wrongs and rescue distressed damsels, like in the troubadour songs."

"Then you had better pay more attention to your sword practice," Tom answered.

They reached the modest house where the Dobbins family gathered. It resembled no other, neither hut, cottage, nor mansion, but the dwelling of a freeholder in the midst of the vast domain of the earl. The owner of the island of property stood beside the baron and lady, head up rather than bent in submission.

Old Tom Dobbins' reputation as a character had good grounds. The stories came down from other grandfathers that he had been a noble knight himself at one time, had come from the north with his dark, beautiful wife and purchased his freehold with gold. Gwenlian Dobbins still had traces of the legendary beauty as she watched from a doorway. She would speak no Norman French or Anglo-Saxon English, but she understood both. Her husband and grandchildren spoke her native Welsh, but Tom's mother, peering over her shoulder now, had trouble communicating.

"You were a good commander to my son who died in your service," Old Tom said to the earl. "I'll not say you Nay if the lad wants to take your penny.

It is up to him." He turned to the women at the house, who answered each in her own tongue to his explanation. Again he spoke to Henry de Bohun. "It is time young Tom went out on his own. He has brothers enough to keep the place."

Earl Bohun looked down at the quiet face of young Tom Dobbins. "Will you enter service with me, lad? You will be trained as a man-at-arms like your father, but your fealty will be to this wrongheaded son of mine, who is always in trouble—never intentionally, of course."

Tom looked up at William, who grinned in delight. The dark boy nodded. "It would be easier to keep an eye on him if I were sworn to him and had no other duties."

"Then come to the castle before evening, and we will draw up a paper for your grandfather to hold."

The commoners bent to Earl Henry in farewell, which he acknowledged with a careless wave.

William bounced in his saddle while his pony rolled an annoyed eye. "Oh, Tom! We will have such fun!"

"You will!" the lad curtly replied. "I will be worn to a frazzle watching you."

"It won't be that bad, Tom. You will remind me of my duty before I get into difficulties. Do you really not want to be my man?"

The boy looked so woeful that Tom almost smiled. The glimmer brightened his dark face.

"Of course I do. I should have chosen work two years ago if it were not for wanting to follow you. You're the most entertainment I have ever had."

"No one would know it from looking at you. Why

don't you smile more?"

An outright grin flashed and disappeared. "I learned quite young that most people do not like to be laughed at, and that it is best to keep my feelings to myself."

William shook his fist at Tom. "Do you laugh at me?"

"A dozen times a day."

The lad dropped his hand. "Oh, well," he sighed, "I will just have to stand it."

Tom turned back to a final meal with his family while his new master rode on to the gaping gate of the castle. There William jumped off the pony, leaving it to anyone who chanced to take it to the stable. Handing Beauty to a page, he ran up the steps to the long hall.

"His grace wants you in the ladies' chamber, where the others of the family gather," the page called after him.

William nodded. He hastily changed his horse-odor garments for those suitable for a formal meeting with his parents.

The ladies' chamber, called a solar, occupied the top of a high tower, bright with windows. A parapet sheltered them from any possible crossbow bolt, allowing entrance only to friendly sunshine. The walls hung solidly with tapestries woven and embroidered by the women of the household. Their working frames, complete with new projects, stood against the wall, while the family gathered near the fireplace. The March chill called for extra heat even here in the solar.

"Willie!" A bright-faced 10-year-old girl ran to

him, her skirts flying immodestly. "Do you know why our father wants to speak to us? Only we who are of reasoning years? Of course, not the little ones!"

Their mother, still pale and tired from the birth of the youngest of many children, had to smile. "Margaret, if you do not quiet yourself we will assume that you are not of reasoning years and send you to the nursery."

"But, Mamma, what is it?"

All the youngsters listened intently in case of a possible clue. But all they got was a shake of the head and a strange expression—was it fear?—that crossed their mother's face.

Not one servant attended, a circumstance so unusual that it made all the young people silent, from Eleanor, in her young ladyhood, Humphrey, Alice, and William to little Margaret. The door curtain swung aside to admit Lady Margaret, followed by Earl Henry de Bohun.

"You had a messenger from Bristol," Lady Maude whispered, her countenance growing still paler.

"Hugh le Brun still lives, thanks to the intercession of Queen Isabella." The man stopped, glancing in turn to each one of his children around the circle. "Margaret, my daughter, I fear you are too young to understand how serious this talk will be. We are in danger as a family, and a loose tongue could cause the death of us all."

The silence seemed almost painful.

"I can hold my tongue better than William," Margaret announced eagerly.

William felt a hot blush creep from neck to hairline. "That is true," he admitted. "She never tells secrets."

A faint smile softened the grimness of his father's face. "Thank you for your courage in admitting this fault. Then Margaret may stay.

"All of you know that our Humphrey is betrothed to the daughter of Raoul de Lusignan, count of Eu, in France. Do you also realize that Count Raoul's older brother, Hugh, is imprisoned at Bristol? With the threat of losing his head? Do you know why?"

Again he surveyed his family in dead silence. "Good, I see you can keep still. King John stole Hugh's betrothed from him, and when Brown Hugh went to war over it, he was defeated, his allies killed, and he himself displayed in chains all over King John's French territory, finally to be made captive at Bristol Castle. If we were wise we would end the betrothal of our son to Hugh's niece. However, we are not so wise. If one member of our family speaks a word of criticism of our lord king, it could mean death not for just him or her, but all of us."

His words echoed heavily in the silent chamber. The family knew that King John had favored their father. Three years before, the king had made Henry the earl of Hereford, and warden of the Welsh Marches, which guarded England from the perennial Welsh raiders. For four generations Bohuns had manned Offa's Dyke* and the border, but never

---

*Offa's Dyke: an earthen wall against the Welsh.

with such rank and favor. Was it worth it to risk all this? The family knew John's fickleness. He changed his mind as easily as his garments.

"Eleanor goes to court soon as a lady-in-waiting to Queen Isabella." Henry looked with approval at his eldest daughter. "Alice must go in a year or two. They will not have an easy life. But I believe them to be discreet and wise for their years."

The girls blushed at his unusual compliment.

"Humphrey, you have been riding with me along the border. Some day, if you live, it will be your responsibility to hold these marches for England. I believe that you are capable of doing it. I cannot leave this area with the raiders stirring, so I wish to send someone on an errand of importance. Humphrey, will you go?"

Only 15 years old, Humphrey had a man's height, needing only to fill out. Already he could wear a man's dignity. "Of course!" he answered proudly.

Henry de Bohun nodded and turned to his mother.

"I have conceived a great desire to visit in France," Lady Margaret assured them. "Before I grow too old! My brother of Scotland sends word that friends of my youth visit there, so it is a good time to go while France and England have an interval of peace. Will you escort me, Humphrey?"

Her grandson looked startled. "To France? Oh, yes!"

William felt a sinking feeling in his stomach. No chance of anyone's trusting *him* with a secret mission. Would he never learn to think before he spoke or acted, so he could stand tall and quiet and accept a charge the way his brother could? He drew a big breath and let it out so loudly he attracted his father's attention. All eyes turned to him.

"I don't suppose——" Henry reflected. Then he addressed the grandmother. "You wouldn't want to bother with William."

"Why not?" Lady Margaret answered. "If Tom Dobbins is with us."

William feared he would start crying. What breath he had came short and quick. His eyes thanked his grandmother, and she winked quickly at him.

She was his favorite relative. Except, of course, sometimes his stern father was admirable, if not lovable. And his mother was comfortable to have around when he did not feel well. His breathing grew more manageable and he thought, Wait until I tell Tom! Then, No, I must be reserved and let my father do that.

Tom Dobbins came to the great hall just before the gates closed for the night. His grandfather, who accompanied him, had much the same build, though a "ruff" of white framed his face.

"Well, Tom," Earl Henry addressed the older man, "you insist on a beard yet!"

The other man stroked his facial adornment. "Only those who can do it well should." He eyed the earl's bare chin. The clerk drew near with parchment, ink, and quill.

"Let's get on with it, Young Henry," said the old man.

William looked with surprise at his father.

Young Henry! From Old Tom Dobbins it did not constitute disrespect.

The clerk quickly wrote the dictated document. So many suits of clothing suitable to the circumstances. Food, bed, weapons, mounts—all to be supplied. So much money per year in gold. Training as a man-at-arms, in crossbowmanship, in swordplay, and more. There seemed no end to the conditions.

Finally the clerk handed the quill to Henry, who passed it on to William. The boy reddened as he laboriously traced out "Wm d'Bohun." To his surprise, Tom took the quill and looked at his grandfather.

"Your true name," the older man said.

Tom bent and inscribed "Thos d'Aubynes." The witnesses, Henry de Bohun and Thomas d'Aubynes, signed both copies, one for Bohun records and one for the Dobbins family.

"Hold your hands out, William," Earl Henry prompted. For the first time William received the oath of fealty. Tom knelt before him and placed palms together between William's hands while the fair Norman reddened with emotion.

"I swear loyalty to my lord, William de Bohun, to serve him, shield and guard him, until death or until my lord releases me."

Then came William's turn to speak. "I swear to be a good lord, fulfilling all my responsibilities toward my man, Thomas Dobbins, until death or until we both agree on release."

Pulling Tom to his feet, William put an arm around the broad shoulders. "You know he is my friend, too?" The boys faced their guardians almost defiantly.

Earl Henry and Old Tom nodded at each other.

"You will do," Henry stated.

Old Tom cuffed his grandson lightly on the ear. "You too. Goodbye, son." He swung around and marched off.

# Chapter Two

The earl of Hereford ceremoniously assisted his mother to her thronelike saddle. It embodied what comfort one could have on horseback. The packhorses vanished through the gate while a sturdy band of men-at-arms waited outside for those now mounting.

"A large-enough escort to discourage any interference, but not large enough to seem a threat to the landholders you pass," Henry explained. "And if all else fails, my mother, look at the intruders the way you used to at me when I erred as a youngster."

Lady Margaret laughed. "It has been a long time since I employed that look on you, Henry. Behave yourself. I want to see you when I return."

On the ladies' walk, far above, William's mother may have shed a few tears, but her sons had not seen them. A filmy scarf, then three, waved from high on the tower.

William swung his cap at them, and then pulled it back on to cover his ears snugly. His grandmother was already cold, he could tell by her reddened nose, but she would never admit it. The party filed out to join their escort and Fra Anselm, Lady Margaret's chaplain.

The river Wye smiled in the sunshine, flowing serenely between its green banks, untroubled by the chill wind. A blue tit winged by them, his brilliant color extinguished suddenly amid the green of a thicket, and his scolding *dee-dee-dee* followed them. The hills to the east still hid the sun, but even touched by first rays, the mountains to the southwest appeared black. Over there, beyond Offa's Dyke, the Welsh waited, often deceptively peaceful, but ready for any inattention by the warden of the Marshes.

"You speak Welsh, don't you, Tom?"

The dark youth reined his horse a little closer. His dark new garb of a man-at-arms became him. He wore the blue-and-silver Bohun badge proudly. Over his shoulder a strap supported quiver and crossbow. Having surprised his instructor at his skill with them, he already had "graduated" from that class.

"Yes, of course. My grandmother will speak nothing else."

"Your grandfather is Norman, and your mother English. With all those languages, you should be useful."

"And your grandmother taught you the Scottish tongue. Between us, we could overhear quite a lot, my lord."

"Will you stop my-lording me?"

The dark face remained still, but the eyes twinkled. "Yes, my lord!—Willie."

William groaned. "I suppose you have to call me 'my lord' when anyone is around, but I'll put up with 'Willie' when we're alone."

He looked back at the castle. Beyond, Hereford Town lay with its unfinished cathedral towering above the walls. He sighed. "I wish I could have brought Beauty. She would enjoy all this travel."

"It is almost time to free her to find a mate and raise young ones," Tom replied. "You would not want to let her go in France. And she might be seasick on the voyage."

The boys glanced again toward Wales. "Tom, have you ever been over the mountains with your Welsh relatives?"

The other lad's face seemed stonier than ever. "My Welsh relatives cast off my grandmother for marrying a Norman. I would be welcome with neither Welsh nor Norman family."

"But now it's getting respectable to intermarry. Anyway that is not what I asked. Have you ever been over?"

A gleam from the dark eyes showed hidden mirth.

"Come on, Tom. Tell me about it. I know they do not really eat babies! Are they good people, like others?"

"Good and bad, like anyone else. They object to being overrun and forced to give up their ancient Christianity for the Roman Church. If the Normans let them alone and quit crowding, they would be peaceable."

William remained thoughtful for a long time.

The party forsook the main trail to bypass Gloucester. "We need not advertise our travels," Lady Margaret remarked. "Though we have another reason, too. Fra Anselm has bespoken a lodging for us at a small abbey. Cells for each of us with one attendant, and the men will camp within a walled enclosure."

The cells for visitors contained little beyond room to roll out bedding, and a crucifix on the wall, but the walls shut out the wind, and the hot food warmed the body. At one side of the abbey a narrow door let the monks carry a pail of soup and a basket of bread to the thin-faced people waiting outside.

"Times are hard," sighed Fra Anselm. "Times are always hard for some. No wonder many poor people go on Crusade. Their debts are forgiven if they take the cross, and if they die on the way, they have been promised forgiveness of sins and a sure place in heaven."

"It has been years since King Richard's Crusade," William said.

"A new one is abuilding in France," the monk told them. "Almost three years ago Fulk of Neuilly started preaching that it was a shame for Christians to worship in Jerusalem or Bethlehem only by courtesy of heathens."

"Three years? And they have not started yet?"

"It takes much time to prepare such an army. Think of the food, the ships, the armor, and the weapons they must obtain. Much money, many men to recruit. Their first leader, the young Thibaut, died. Now they have chosen a new one, and the pace quickens."

The next day they passed Malmesbury Abbey. Fra Anselm sighed because he wished to halt for several days to read the histories William of Malmesbury had written there, but they had to hurry on.

Another day they saw the great stones on Salisbury Plain. Fra Anselm crossed himself, sure as many were that only the devil could set up such monstrous rocks.

"I'd like to have seen him do it!" William

exclaimed, rising from his saddle to see them better.

"Can't you be interested without telling all the world?" Tom urged him.

So William attempted to prove he could keep still across miles and miles of drab, uninteresting territory. Things picked up half a day from the coast.

"Praise God that we have Tom Dobbins," Lady Margaret sighed to Humphrey. "This is the third time Tom has brought William back from following a dancing bear or a juggler. Let us be gone as fast as possible."

Only two hundred miles of sea separated them from their landing in France, but miles mean nothing if winds will otherwise. Instead of a couple of days, the passage took a week. Not only Lady Margaret and her woman but most of the party came down with seasickness. William tried the patience of the sailors with his urge to know everything. Tom followed him about, grimly determined not to allow water—even heaving water—to cause him to abandon his charge.

"Tom, lie down, do!" William demanded. "You look terrible, sort of greenish tan."

"Thanks. Will you lie down too?"

"Well, no. I have to see how they unship the mast. The captain says the wind blows too fast, though finally in the right direction."

Manfully Tom held back a groan and went to watch the mast laid flat.

Land looked so good, even to William, when it finally showed on the horizon.

"Soon Le Tréport, our goal!" he announced

happily to his party.

Lady Margaret gave him a glance of loathing. As the sheltered water calmed, she rose shakily. "What I endure for my family!" Tom heard her murmur.

Fra Anselm and the captain went to find and buy horses while the others discovered that the land seemed more unsteady than the water. William almost staggered over the edge of the wharf. The liquid below, thick with garbage, would not have made for happy swimming.

Tom carried several of William's bundles. Though they did not travel in state, yet the group had to provide all its needs. Hospitality could not extend to furnishing beds for such a cavalcade, even in the greatest houses.

Now they would visit one of those great houses. When they reached the town of Eu, travelers filled the streets, men-at-arms wearing the badges of many masters. William's party noted blue-and-white ones similar to the Bohun colors.

"Of the house of Champagne," Lady Margaret exclaimed in more excited tones than William had yet heard from her. "One of the younger branches."

"It is so like ours," William puzzled.

She nodded. "Because you are distantly related. The light-blue background of the shield and the slanted band of silver or white are common among kinsmen of Champagne. Humphrey, you must plan a distinguishing design to add to your shield so you may be recognized when you are in full armor."

Humphrey sat taller in the saddle. His plain blue-and-white shield had formerly seemed adequate, but his thoughts were now almost visible as he watched the various badges.

The castle bailey* seemed packed with armed men. The mayor of the castle received with consternation the message sent from Lady Margaret. The place already overflowed, and where would he put a princess? And the betrothed of the daughter of the house?

Servants led Lady Margaret and her attendants and Humphrey and William into the great hall. Here they saw silks and jewels and Eastern styles unknown in western England. Those returning from earlier Crusades had brought such extravagances back that they had changed the dress of Europe. The English Normans felt quite drab beside their hosts.

The mayor slipped through the crowd to the dais and the couple enthroned there, where he whispered urgently in the lord's ear. In turn, Count Raoul spoke to his wife. The two stood while the mayor sped back to Lady Margaret and the boys.

"Lady Princess Margaret of Scotland and Bohun. Lord Humphrey Bohun! William de Bohun!"

The babble among the visitors died away when the count and countess of Eu stood, so all heard the announcement. A path opened before the Bohuns, and they approached the two who eagerly awaited them. William, trailing behind his brother and grandmother, knew that the anxiety was not for his family, but for the news they surely brought of

---
*bailey: a castle courtyard

Brown Hugh.

Ceremonious greetings took time, and William soon grew bored with them. He tried to control his fidgets. Some of the noble lords present bore names that even he knew.

Simon de Montfort* wore his red-and-white colors with such dignity and consciousness of worth that he stood out even among the other greats. Many in the streets had worn the white fork-tailed lion on red of Montfort.

The colors of Peter of Amiens showed on a number of the throng. He, of course, was a near neighbor.

Conan of Béthune had a lute slung on his back, and William remembered that he was one of the great troubadours.† A lord and knight on his own account, he was also attached to the great count of Flanders, whose power exceeded that of kings.

Standing behind Humphrey's chair, William prepared to enjoy the music beginning across the hall. "I sing not of the stars or moon or rippling rills," Conan's voice rose. "I sing only of the sunshine of my lady's smile." The boy could also hear the low-toned conversation going on at the high table.

Lady Alix, countess of Eu, asked with a catch of breath, "Our Hugh in a dungeon? After all the humiliations John heaped on him in France!"

Lady Margaret assured her that the jailers made his cell as comfortable as possible, for they had

---
*Montfort: father of the famous Montfort of England
†troubadours: singers of love songs

great (though necessarily unexpressed) sympathy for the wronged man.

"But no sunshine for wild, fierce Hugh," sorrowed his brother. "Your son, Lady Margaret, is high in favor. We cannot understand how he remains so when our families are linked by betrothal."

Humphrey, youngest of those at the high table, made bold to speak. "The king wishes a strong baron to hold the western marches. Bohuns have done better at such than at mincing and prancing at court. We breakfast at five o'clock in the morning at Hereford Castle, not noon."

Lady Alix pretended to swoon, bringing a laugh from those nearby. "Oh, my poor child!" she faintly exclaimed. "Do not, I beg of you, expect such early rising here."

Humphrey grinned and apologized. "The ladies do as they please about rising time at Hereford Castle, so do not be alarmed for your daughter."

Bells sounded for evening prayers. The voices of the knights and lords hushed. Since they were too many for the little chapel, they knelt where they were

Abbot Martin, one of the knightly ecclesiastics who preached Crusade, led the prayer. "Our Lord Christ, send us quickly on the way to redeem Jerusalem by our arms from the hold of the heathen."

Most of the men present wore the white cross symbolizing their pledge to the new Crusade. William felt a great thrill of pride to be present when the cause of God was forwarded. He would like to have a share in it—but how could a boy be a help? His birthday came soon, but even at 13 he could expect only to go as a page to some noble house for training in courtly ways.

The count and countess of Eu had ordered one floor of a tower cleared of its residents to house Lady Margaret and her entourage. The hangings divided the one room into chambers, one for women and one for her grandsons and their attendants and the chaplain. Tom led them to their beds and placed himself across the doorway at the narrow spiral of stairs in the wall. The floor above held still another visiting household.

The early risers from England woke with dawn, and the two lads slipped out as quietly as they could, to ascend the stairway to a narrow walkway inside the battlements crowning the roof. William leaned out an archer's slot. "Only the kitchen crew moving yet, and a few sleepy sentries. I am glad the cooks are stirring."

"Our Willie is growing. He needs his breakfast." Humphrey had approached unnoticed. "It is Lord Montfort who has the upper floor!"

William ignored the first part of his brother's speech. "I like Lord Montfort. He is what a real knight should be."

His brother nodded, but his abstracted look made his blond brother ask, "What is bothering you, Hump?"

He got a scowl in answer to the nickname. "Don't call me that. I've got some dignity to maintain here!"

Submissively but with a twinkle, William

bowed. "Yes, my lord Humphrey. What worries your lordship?"

His lordship aimed a threatening fist at him, but grinned. "I am thinking about my coat of arms. It is all the style nowadays to have one instead of real things like a Scottish thistle or a sprig of the Anjou heath, the 'Plantagenista.' Grandmother suggests combining the Bohun blue-and-silver with the lion of Scotland. Help me to trace it." Immensely flattered to be in his brother's confidence, William knelt by the drift of dust he indicated. Humphrey drew a shield and slanted the bend* of silver across it with the one-sided scalloped border distinctive to Bohun.

"Where would you put the lion?" William asked. "Are you going to have him rampant, up clawing the air?"

Even Humphrey paid attention when Tom looked at them and said, with a slow shake of the head, "The rampant lion belonged to Richard. Be careful."

"You are right," Humphrey nodded. "King John is jealous of any sign of preference for his older brother. How about three small lions not rampant, but slipping up on the enemy on all fours, their tails curved over their backs and full face to the foe? Here and here and here, across the blue and silver?"

"Tremendous," William replied. "Not like anyone else, and hard to forget."

The boys rose, dusting their knees.

---

*bend: a diagonal stripe

## Chapter Three

*H*umphrey looked at his dusty self with disapproval. "After we eat, we are to go as a family to a formal meeting with my betrothed, so stir yourself, Willie. Then there is a grand meeting at the cathedral for a sermon by Abbot Martin on the sins of this generation, which the new crusade of Pope Innocent will help to vanquish, supposedly. A busy day."

"Have you seen Lady Maude de Eu, Hump?"

His brother failed to notice the hated nickname. "Just for a moment. She's all right, I suppose."

Then he vanished down the stairs. The other boys exchanged glances.

"I'm sorry," William said, "for the girl who has to go away to marry someone she doesn't know, and maybe never see her family again. Maybe it is to someone who will be cruel to her. Suppose her husband does not like her? No wonder she is scared. Not everyone is like our Eleanor, who could give as good as she gets, or my grandmother, who told her new husband that if he did not treat her right, she would walk home!"

"She had not the sea between her and her family," Tom answered as he led the way down.

Humphrey's mother had carefully coached him as to the way to greet his prospective bride. He presented a picture of chivalry and devotion as he went to a knee and kissed her hand. The girl's frightened look gradually gave way to rosy pleasure.

Other family members talked among themselves, giving the young people time to get acquainted. William looked from the deep slot of window into the bailey, where the knights going on Crusade prepared for their entrance into the cathedral. Each wore the white cross on the left shoulder and upper arm.

"Quite a number of them received their crosses from the hand of Fulk of Neuilly, the priest who began calling for repentance and purging of sins through Crusade," his grandmother commented as she watched also. "Many will not return. Young, strong men and grayheads, they are all afire to reclaim Jerusalem."

William gave a great sigh. "I wish I could see them in tournament, showing their skills."

Countess Margaret sniffed. "A waste of lives! As the Holy Father said when he banned tournaments for five years, far better that they spend their lives for God's cause than for self and pride. Pride is the sin of our age—or any other age, for that matter."

William did not seem convinced, nor did his mournful expression abate, but nothing could be done about holding a tournament.

A laugh from Little Lady Maude caught his attention. Humphrey must be charming her after all.

"Madam Grandmother, we have been planning a coat of arms." William had her full attention. The boy described their idea.

"Excellent! Except possibly for yours, a silver chief* with a lioncel† like Humphrey's on it."

---

*chief: a band across the top of a coat of arms
†lioncel: a small lion

"A shield for me? Oh, Grandmother!"

"Come," she said, smiling. "Let us find our cousins of Eu and ask if their clerk can draw up the designs in color so we may see them as they will really appear."

The priestly chaplain-clerk of the castle showed his pleasure at the request. He did Humphrey's first on a fine sheet of vellum, then William's, with the boy tiptoe in excitement.

A page came running to summon them to the cathedral. The vast, shadowy interior resembled the vaulted gloom of a mighty forest, branches from the columns meeting far above. Chill gray stone, shafts of light from high windows, and the small points of candle flames combined in awesome effect.

Worshipers filled the sides, then the Crusaders strode slowly in, rank upon rank, each lord with his knights behind him. William's heart rose in his throat, choking him. All those valiant men ready to give their lives for the cause of Christ! The ritual of kneeling, rising, chants, and responses built the tension. The abbot's small figure, so dwarfed by the stone canopy over his high lectern, did not seem little long. His voice filled the church.

"Ye are sinners deserving of death."

"Amen," whispered through columns and coves.

"Ye are filled with evil desires and licentiousness!"

"Amen" came the soft reply.

"What have you done that would make you worthy of eternal life?"

"Nothing. Nothing. Nothing."

"Our Lord Christ sets before you a work that will elevate you from the pit of your lusts."

"Amen!" Now the response rang clear.

He brought the congregation to such a height of emotion that they could not control their sobs. Tears ran down not only satin cheeks but shaven faces, as well, and mingled with drooping moustaches.

William could hardly bear it. "I will go, Lord Christ—let me go!" he whispered softly. How could he go when he was not yet 13 (and subject to errors of judgment)?

On their knees the great throng listened to the soprano voices of the boy choir, and the ancient words of Saint Andrew of Crete, now so applicable:

"Christian, dost thou see them on the holy ground?
 How the powers of darkness compass thee around?
 Christian, up and smite them, counting gain but loss
 In the strength that cometh by the holy cross.

"Christian, dost thou feel them, how they work within,
 Striving, tempting, turning, goading into sin?
 Christian, never tremble, never be downcast.
 Gird thee for the battle, watch and pray and fast.

"Christian, dost thou hear them, how they

speak thee fair?
'Always fast and vigil! Always watch and prayer!'
Christian, answer boldly, 'While I breathe, I pray!'
Peace shall follow battle, night shall end in day.

" 'Well I know thy trouble, O my servant true.
Thou art very weary. I was weary too.
But that trial shall make thee someday all mine own.
At the end of sorrow, thou shalt be near my throne.' "

The crusaders withdrew, the martial sound of their feet only a little less fast than the pounding of William's heart.

Humphrey's face was an alarming white. "I cannot go. My father needs me on the Welsh Marches, where the dark little men wait for a moment of inattention," he whispered.

Lady Maude's rosiness gave way to pallor, then rushed back when she realized the meaning of his words. He would not go on the desperate Crusade. Then she hung her head, embarrassed at her selfishness.

Lady Margaret eyed William, who walked in a daze. "This," she said briskly, "will be repeated at St. Pol and Béthune on the way to join Baldwin of Flanders. It is very effective."

William did not hear. He stumbled over a cobblestone, and Tom quickly took his arm.

The count and countess of Eu had quite a bit to

say about Jerusalem. His uncle, Guy of Lusignan, had been king of Jerusalem, placed there by Richard of England and Normandy, until pushed out by the Saracens. He then endured some time in imprisonment, and after his release he had died on the island of Cyprus.

"Are you not impressed to join the Crusade?" Humphrey asked his host.

"The need is great here. We are vassals of Philip of France and cannot know when England's John may break treaty and attack us from Normandy. Especially with so many brave men leaving. We have contributed to the arming of poor knights who could not afford their own armor, and to feeding the chivalry who do go."

Lady Alix bore an anxious look. "I fear for the countless number of common people who follow Fulk. He means to lead them over the Alps to Venice, and they are not prepared. While he has collected much money to feed them, their numbers will overwhelm the countryside. There is not enough food to buy for such a multitude."

"They believe that God will create a miracle such as that of the loaves and fishes," her husband answered.

"Count Baldwin is providing shipping for the chivalry, horse and man, to round Spain and go by sea to Venice," Lady Margaret added. "Venice is building ships to carry all from there to the Holy Land."

The whole mealtime William sat in silence. A frown crinkled his grandmother's forehead as she observed him. Tom, seated at the lowest table, also watched his charge. As the knights retired to ready themselves for a long ride to St. Pol, the older boy caught his young lord's arm. "Are you sick?" he demanded.

William's eyes were heavy with misery. "I don't know. I want to take the cross so badly I feel sick at my stomach."

Later Lady Margaret found a moment to corner Tom. "Is what ails the boy what I think it is?"

"He wants to go with the knights on Crusade."

"Always, always! His ambition is always larger than his abilities."

Tom faced her with his quiet, steadfast eyes. "Why should William return to England? Unless he must take the place of Humphrey if that one dies, he must make his own way somewhere. Who knows? It may be in the Holy Land. England is not safe for noble sons just now."

"You are willing to go with him? You're as bad as he!"

"No, my lady, I count the cost before I venture."

She turned suddenly to sweep from the room, and the swish of her skirts faded down the spiral stairs.

That evening William lay on his pallet, face to the wall. Tom waited silently for Lady Margaret's return while the rush lights flickered and died one by one. It must have been an hour before she came up the staircase with a faint waver of light preceding her from the wick floating in a cup of grease. She held it up to see Tom and her woman servant rising to greet her.

"I talked to Simon de Montfort and our hosts,"

she announced. "Simon will stay to talk to William. We will see." And she shrugged.

Her grandson, his head buried in his arms, neither saw nor heard her.

Simon de Montfort had a sternness about him but could dissolve unexpectedly into laughter. Knights had great respect for the 35-year-old baron and knew they could go to him in confidence for even small matters.

A page summoned William to appear before the lord. The latter's young son leaned so confidingly against his father's shoulder that the English boy for a moment lost some of his anxiety. William wondered why Lord Montfort had not gone on with his comrades in arms.

Under the baron's searching eyes, the boy felt smaller, slighter, younger, than ever. Tom stood a pace or so behind him, though it was no scrape for Tom's rescuing hand to intervene in. Still it was comforting to have him there.

"How is your health, Young Bohun?"

William's eyes widened. "Very good, I think."

"You look as if you had no sleep last night. Were you sick?"

A dull red crept up under the boy's fair skin. "I—just could not sleep."

"Why?"

A long silence ended only when the boy realized that Montfort would insist on an answer. Apologetically he spoke. "I thought of Christ's homeland in the hands of infidels who mock pilgrims, and I wanted to do something about it—and cried because I am too young." His words ended in a rush, almost defiantly. Another silence followed, which William himself broke.

"Men do cry!"

Montfort nodded. "What are your skills?"

William drew a deep breath. "I am a good rider and can take care of my own horse. I practice swordplay every day with Tom. Of course, my sword isn't a large one. I'm not big enough yet to handle a long lance, but I am growing." He thought a moment. "And I see things."

The baron raised an eyebrow. "So? What kind of things?"

The lad looked appealingly at Tom. "Just—things."

Stepping forward, Tom bowed, waiting permission to speak. Montfort nodded again. "He sees what others often miss, sire. Birds, animals, the way people act and feel. And secrets, which he does not tell."

"How do you know?"

"Because I go where he goes. That is my commission."

Amusement spread across Simon's face. "So it is a case of two or none."

With a rather childish wriggle William answered the baron's smile. "He teaches me to look before I leap, and is most useful."

"Would you allow *him* to come with me on Crusade?" Montfort asked.

William's smile disappeared, followed by an expression of paper-white anguish. That in turn smoothed into a kind of stony calm. "If that is the best way I could help win back the Holy Land from the Saracens, yes."

"H'mmm. You may go, but I want to see you again."

As he blindly headed for the door, William bumped into Tom. They climbed to the tower roof, where they could see the last of the column of Crusaders winding upriver, north and east to St. Pol. Neither boy could say anything comforting to the other, so they watched the departing knights.

Finally a diminutive page stumbled up the steps. "Baron de Montfort wants you now."

They hardly felt like hurrying, but made their feet obey anyway. Not only Simon awaited them but Lady Margaret and Humphrey, who looked grim.

"William," his grandmother told him, "Simon de Montfort requests that you be allowed to attend him."

The boy suddenly found himself out of breath, unable to make a sound. Tom's eyes narrowed, his usual sole sign of amusement.

Montfort cleared his throat. "I had not intended to take a page, which seems to be the only position open. Still, I could use one who has wide-open eyes. However, few pages have squires to attend them." Attempting to frown at his new page, he inquired, "What do we do about that?"

"He—he can see anything that I miss," William offered, his voice ragged with unbelieving hope.

Simon rose. "You will remain here to be suitably equipped. After your brother is invested as a knight, you will ride to catch up with me. Your escort will then bring back my son, who will be with me until then."

"Thank you, sire," the lad managed to whisper. Not until the baron had disappeared did he think back over what he had heard.

"Hump! Are you really to receive your knighthood?"

His brother nodded quickly and walked off.

Lady Margaret permitted herself a small smile. "William, your brother is of two minds. One is glad and proud to be approved for knighthood by several of the lords, who have entrusted that honoring to Count Raoul. His other mind is disturbed because his young brother is to receive, so young! an honor almost as great from Simon de Montfort. He had almost rather had your appointment than his own. We will worry about you, dear one, but Humphrey is truly not unhappy about it. It's just that he cannot resolve his feelings quite yet."

"You did it, didn't you, Grandmother Princess!" William's face glowed. "Oh, thank you, thank you!"

# Chapter Four

William's breathless delight in being fitted with light armor almost provoked Tom into a smile. The armor consisted of small links knitted together so they looked like a coarse sweater of knee length, divided front and back to permit him to ride horseback. The undergarment of soft doeskin protected his skin from chafing. Tom helped pull the armor over the boy's head, and as William's flushed face emerged laughing from the neck, the squire's mouth came even closer to a smile.

"Be careful, Tom, you almost smiled!"

The squire of Count Raoul glanced briefly at the dark boy whose grimness made him seem much older than his young lord. But he noticed nothing different about his expression.

"Now for the basinet,"* he said, returning to his task. He tried one, then another, of the new lightweight head coverings, deep bowl-shaped, with a narrow plate extending between the eyes to protect the nose. "This one will do. First a padded leather cap, then the hood of links, with a curtain to the shoulders for neck protection. Finally the basinet. This will not protect you from an ax blow or the slash of a great broadsword, but it will help save you from minor cuts."

At last came the overtunic, blue, with a white bend. On the left shoulder bloomed the white cross of this Crusade. The red-and-white badge of Lord

---

*basinet: a light steel medieval helmet

Simon adorned the breast.

Humphrey entered as the two squires fastened the links under his brother's chin. Then they girded the lad's own light sword on him. He turned to face his brother and waited for comment. It was slow coming. The older boy looked him over carefully before he spoke.

"Very well. But you lack gauntlets." Drawing a pair of supple gloves from his belt, he held them for William to slide his hands into. The palms and fingers were as soft as leather could be and still take wear. The backs of the hands and the flared cuffs were of heavy oxhide, as tough as steel. "Wear them in honor, brother."

Suddenly William asked, "Who pays for all this? I never thought——"

Although Humphrey's lifted eyebrows said, When did you ever? he did not voice it. "That is between our grandmother and the count of Eu. You may thank them both."

The chain mail seemed heavy. It would take time to get used to it. "How about Tom?" asked William.

The dark boy rejected the offer of mail. "I will wear toughened oxhide, breast, back, and shoulder plates, but would be glad for one of the new basinets."

"Tom must wear my badge as well as Lord Montfort's. Like this." William drew a shield with the lower half Bohun blue-and-silver, upper half red with a white, fork-tailed lioncel. "See?"

Tom made a warlike figure with his dark garments setting off his shining helmet, crossbow and bolt case on his back, and bright badges on shoulder and breast. Even Humphrey showed respect, though he had other matters on his mind.

"Cub," he addressed William, "will you pray with me all night before the cathedral altar? I am to keep vigil tonight in preparation for the ceremony tomorrow."

Forgetting his own pomp and dignity, he caught Humphrey's hand. "Oh, brother, may I? Thank you, Hump!"

He received a cuff for the nickname, but the blow hurt Humphrey more than William. Still, the force of that fist staggered the younger boy.

"I forgot," William told him repentantly. "I forgot your new dignity, Lord Humphrey."

Silent knights, all in armor, escorted the Bohun heir to the gloomy depths of the cathedral. Watching closely his own behavior as page lest he disgrace the family, William followed in his train. He admired Humphrey's calm as the noble attendants divested him of all his clothing and robed him in plain white for the night of prayer.

William had tried to sleep in the afternoon, unsuccessfully, as a preparation. But he felt no sleepiness now in the hollow echoes of the almost empty building. Humphrey knelt in silent prayer as the various hours passed, each with its contingent file of monks to intone the suitable chants, then leave. Although William tried to imitate his brother's stillness, it was difficult. Once he woke to find his head supported by a step, and stealthily regained his knees.

Somewhere in the depths of the high-arched nave, Tom knelt too. The thought comforted the younger boy. The knights who supported Humphrey had not seemed to notice William's lapse. He tried to keep his mind on Humphrey, praying that he would always be a faithful, true knight. (Some who performed those vows did not take them seriously.) As for himself, he prayed that he would be a good servant to God and be useful to Count Simon, who had so greatly honored him. For Tom he asked God that others could see what a constant friend the older lad was, more than an ordinary man-at-arms. He prayed that his sister Eleanor, and later Alice, might be discreet in their service to Isabella, queen of the unstable King John. Above all, he prayed that the Crusade would free Jerusalem, now trodden underfoot by the infidels.

Hearing a bird's sleepy chirp, he noticed that the high windows showed a faint trace of light. A larger group of monks filed in for morning prayers. Shortly after came the tread of the armored feet of knights to raise Humphrey and take him to an antechamber. There William held a cloth the lords used to dry Humphrey after bathing him.

Another pair lowered a white tunic over his clean body. They explained the symbolism as they did so. "White for purity in the new life you are to lead."

Others put him into a red vest, signifying the blood he would shed in defense of the helpless and innocent. The blood Christ had shed for him.

Next came the chain mail, topped by shoulder- and breastplates, black as the night of death, which must be hopeless without the death of

Christ on the cross for him.

The great count of Eu girded him with the belt of chastity, and the new scabbarded sword that hung there brought a gasp of admiration from William. It was the gift of Eu to the new knight, as were the glorious inlaid spurs that Raoul knelt to fasten to his feet. "Use them for riding speedily to rescue the innocent. Kneel, Humphrey of Bohun."

As William's brother knelt, his mail rustled, and the vastness of the cathedral magnified the clinking of his spurs. The cylindrical helmet clasped under his arm finished his equipment. His sleek head bent before the silent, stern-faced assembly of knights. Count Raoul lifted his bared great sword and struck lightly the boy's shoulder with the flat of the blade.

"In the name of God, Saint Michael, and Saint Denis, rise, Sir Humphrey."

The grim, unyielding faces about the young knight instantly changed. Grins, comradely buffets on shoulder and back, and hearty handshakes all greeted Sir Humphrey. The crush drove William back to Tom's side.

Ladies now came from the recesses of the cathedral and kissed the cheek of the honored one, who gallantly saluted their hands with such grace as his armor allowed.

Lady Margaret smiled as if she had long been accustomed to doing so. Then, as if realizing her lapse from regal dignity, she sobered.

"One more item before you leave us, William. After Humphrey—Sir Humphrey, I should say— is relieved of his armor, there will be a formal betrothal of Lady Maude to him before the high altar. Since the court is already assembled, now is a good opportunity."

The ceremony had all the force of a legal marriage contract, and while Little Lady Maude would not return with the Bohuns to their marches now, when she did go, it would be as a Bohun, to cross England with all the protection of that great name. The frightened child of their arrival gave Sir Humphrey her hand and her vows with joyful eyes raised to meet his grave regard.

"Now that is over, Tom." William laid his arm over the shoulder of his companion. "We go right after early breakfast tomorrow." He gave an unseemly skip that no one saw but his squire.

Sleepiness overcame the boy long before dark, so he and Tom drowsed in the sunshine on the tower roof. Suddenly William woke from a dream.

"I thought Queen Isabella still lived here and none of the past two years had happened," he told his squire. "She lived here, you know, with Count Raoul and Countess Alix before King John saw her. She should have married Hugh le Brun, Count Raoul's brother. When her parents came for her, the count of Eu had to let her go. Her parents held Angoulême in fief from King John. As the only child and the heiress, she had to go to him to swear fealty."

"H'mm," Tom answered sleepily.

"I don't think it's right to blame Count Raoul for letting her go. You noticed some hard glances from the nobles who left yesterday. They think the count at fault and the cause of the death of those knights who helped Hugh try to get her back. But there was nothing Count Raoul could do about it. No wonder he looks sad so much."

Tom roused himself. "I wonder if we will get to the Isle of Cyprus, where another of the Lusignan uncles is still king. If we retake Jerusalem, Amalric de Lusignan may again assume the throne King Richard gave him in the Holy Land."

The small page scrambled up the stairs on hands and feet, so great was his haste. "Your lady grandmother bids you dress for banquet, Lord William."

The high table had been shortened, but still many knights and a few lords attended. Tonight William, instead of standing at his brother's back, had a seat of honor, with Tom behind him to serve. The waiting men brought trays of food, and his squire chose portions for him, as if William were one of the great ones. It honors the Crusade, he reminded himself silently, not William of Bohun.

A round of speeches and well-wishing followed (during which William grew dreadfully sleepy, though he had to try to look intelligent). Then a stir at the other end of the hall announced a newcomer. He was somewhat more than a man-at-arms, but less than a knight. All of the Bohuns stood, but Lady Margaret seated herself again, waving Humphrey to meet the visitor. "It is Peter, from home!"

The grizzled soldier delivered a packet to Humphrey and came to drop to a knee by the English lady.

"What is the news, Captain Peter?" she queried.

"All is well at Hereford, my lady, but Count Henry sends for Lord Humphrey. He is to return discreetly, at once, and as though from a foray into the mountains after raiders. Lady Eleanor is with Queen Isabella and happy there, but the king demands to see the Bohun heir. King John is at Winchester, so Humphrey must not return by the way you went."

Little Lady Maude turned pale. "Humphrey will not be in danger, will he?"

"Surely not," the great lady soothed, though William did not agree. One could never trust the fickle King John. He hoped his brother could successfully show that the defense of the western marches needed another Bohun.

The questioning eyes of the court followed the family when with gracious permission they withdrew to an anteroom.

"You will travel faster alone, Humphrey," his princess grandmother stated. "I will remain here to visit other relatives and return at leisure. William goes the opposite way."

Peter's bristly eyebrows raised.

She continued. "Our William has taken the cross and goes to join his sponsors, Simon of Montfort and Count Balwin of Flanders. They take ship soon for Venice."

Now the old soldier's brows drew together, but he said nothing.

Lady Margaret, with an unusual show of affection, embraced her grandsons. "We do not know when we will meet again, lads, but give yourselves into the hands of God. Nothing can happen then, save as He permits. As we go our separate ways His angels will be with each of us, and even if we do not meet again, they will keep record."

Humphrey threw his arms around William. "Take care of Tom, Willie." His eyes twinkled at the joke. "We don't want anything to happen to him."

The younger brother laughed. "I will see that his feet keep dry and he eats right."

Old Peter stood to one side, talking to Lady Margaret. She patted his arm. "Lads, here is another who wishes to take the cross!" At William's suspicious look, she said, "Peter has grown gray in Bohun service. His wife is gone, and younger men can take his place. Rather than retire in Hereford to live with his sons, he would follow William to the Holy Land."

"Not to bodyguard you, cub!" Humphrey assured his brother. "Others besides you feel a desire to chase Saracens!"

The younger Bohun felt his color rise at his brother's accurate guess at his feelings. "I will be glad Peter is around." William nodded at the old man. "He used to make willow whistles for me by the river Wye."

A moment of homesickness hit William. How long before he saw again the green banks of Wye?

"Well"—Humphrey drew himself up—"I am off to Tréport. Count Raoul will give me a note to the harbor master, and Peter's second in command goes with me. Four men also, Peter? I will sleep on the ship—perhaps! Be good, Willie!"

The young knight responded to William's fist in his middle with a grin. He stepped out the door to bid farewell to the Count of Eu and his wife and the pale little lady Maude.

"It will not be long, my betrothed. I am looking forward to rowing you on our beautiful river. We Wye men pride ourselves on boating skills, and it is lovely there, with the sweet birdcalls."

She gave him her hand to kiss, wordless, tears about to fall. William drew back, and the maid's parents turned their heads so as not to notice Humphrey wiping them from the girl's cheeks. "Smile, now. I want to remember you smiling." She obliged with a wavery, watery, curve of lips.

"William," his grandmother stated firmly, "I will not see you off in early morning, so this is our farewell. You will always have our prayers. Do not worry about me. I have Fra Anselm and my own servants, and each of our relatives will give us escort to the next place. Possibly I will visit my brother, William the Lion of Scotland, before I return to Hereford. He has not entertained me for many years. Go with God, our Lord Christ, and all the holy angels, to do His will."

Once more she kissed him on the cheek and walked away, back straight and face composed. No tears for her!

Only William returned to the high table, to represent the family alone. He engaged in disjointed and uncomfortable talk, by fits and starts, sudden recalls to courteous attention, and again abstraction. He described Hereford to Lady Maude, trying to take away her desolate look.

"The Wye Valley is green and lovely. Plum thickets are plentiful, and sometimes when the fruit is ripe we make a party and go horseback with sacks to pick them. Then we dry them to use for plum pudding in the winter. Our cathedral is not as nearly finished as yours, but it feels the same. There are mountains in sight of the castle, black against the southwestern sky.

"My mother's solar room is most pleasant. It catches all the sunshine, and on gray days the fireplace makes it bright and cheerful. Our little sisters and brothers will love you. Margaret is 10 now and beginning to put on ladylike airs, but forgets and tears her dress when romping in the orchard. Eleanor and Alice will both be attending Queen Isabella before you come. We have many relatives in England too. The earl of Chester married my grandmother's sister, and Chester is not far. Essex is my uncle, my mother's brother, so you see we have lots of noble families to visit."

The girl's tears had dried, and she listened eagerly, thus missing hearing the commotion when Humphrey rode out. His brother safely gone, William's throat seemed to give out, and he could talk no more.

"Bed, young Crusader," Count Raoul suggested. "Your horses, gear, and escort will be ready before daylight. Bid your brother goodnight, Maude."

Though William did not think he could sleep, he was mistaken.

## Chapter Five

*T*hough the days had grown longer by May, light barely tinged the sky when the lads came down, dressed for travel. Yawning kitchen boys provided cold food for them. The travelers did not intend to camp on the way to St. Pol, so a long, hard ride faced them. But since they had no women's gear to transport and no ladies to complain of tiring, they hoped to make it without stopping. (William laughed to himself. The French did not know his grandmother. If she were going, she would be as fresh as any of the knights at day's end.)

The common people, seeing the dust of the caravan's fast pace, pulled their carts to one side to allow the party free passage. They looked curiously at the bright colors of overtunics, and respectfully at the white shoulder cross.

William's armor and Tom's hardened leather now traveled bundled away in the baggage, but Captain Peter still had his armor on. If the time came that he must lay aside what he had worn for forty years, he would feel undressed. William noted a scar on the shoulder plate and the dent, well hammered out, in Peter's basinet, and he commented on it.

"It was well that I had not taken it off that time." Peter shook his head. "One could not expect the man to enjoy seeing his hayricks burned as punishment for giving roof to one proscribed, even if the fellow was his own brother. Aye," Peter answered William's look of inquiry, "he got away, and all I had was a bruised head. He gave us a lot more trouble, that one."

The boy rubbed stiffened legs when they dismounted for a break and a change of horses. He delighted in the new one for him, a sturdy dapple-gray verging on white. "He seems strong, with plenty of endurance," William told Tom.

"He is your best mount, to ride into St. Pol, the gift of Countess Alix. And he is to go with us to the Holy Land."

William's pleasure expanded as he glanced at his squire's horse. "And yours is a mate to him! Also from the lady?"

"Yes," Tom agreed. "She is the owner of Eu in her own right, so may bestow expensive gifts. Lord Raoul rules through his marriage to her."

Like England, France held many forests and no great population save in the walled cities and villages. The walls did not bar the periodic pestilences, however, and these kept the head count from rising. And the bloody quarrels between neighboring lords and kings, notably John of England and Philip of France, also kept the population low.

The crusade brought a blessing to the land, for the lords dropped their feuding at the desire of the Holy Father. He offered absolution of sins and cancellation of debts to those who took part. Many penniless knights eagerly grasped the opportunity to win fame and loot—and also to get rid of old burdens.

Several of them joined the travelers from Eu, and such an array of armed men discouraged any bandits in the forest from attacking the caravan. The sun sat red on the western horizon when the company clattered into the bailey of Hugh of St. Pol. He waited there to greet them.

"I delayed so that I might have the company of this young man to the next stop, which is Béthune. It will not be such a long ride."

The lord gripped William by the back of the neck with fingers that felt like iron, and shook him a little. "Come in." He motioned to the wide stairs. "My lady waits to greet you."

Montfort's new page glanced at his hands, darkened with horse sweat and dirt from the neck of his mount.

"Water here!" A boy ran to them with a skin to pour a stream for washing. William rinsed his face of dust and pushed back his wet hair before following the lord of St. Pol.

Hugh, with Conan of Béthune, had been Baldwin's envoy to the Venetians. An older man, Lord Hugh was grayer and more grave than most of the Crusaders. William received the honor of a place at table by his lady. The attempt to converse in knightly chivalry almost undid the boy. She mercifully dismissed him to bed before he brought disgrace upon himself.

"Are there disadvantages to being an honored guest, Willie?" Tom's whisper came out of the dark.

"How I dread getting up in the morning," groaned his young master. "I know I will not be able to move."

"I'll move you," Tom cheerfully offered. "And if I can't do it Peter will help."

"Thanks, friend." And William dropped into a well of sleep.

A gray, dreary day greeted the travelers. Peter's moustache, usually so jaunty, drooped dispiritedly. The bright colors of the knights, which delighted the eye in sunshine, were blurred by drizzle or covered like William's with a drab, tightly woven cloak. He pulled the hood forward to keep the drops out of his eyes. The boy had to laugh to himself. One never thought of going on Crusade in the rain. He laughed again, and Hugh of St. Pol heard him.

"Eh, lad?"

"I thought of crusading in the heat of sun or in dust storms, but never of getting so soggy!"

"Three years this has been in the making," Hugh said. "I began to think it a mirage, a phantasm, that would never come to pass. Even the memory of the envoys lying on their faces in St. Mark's Square before ten thousand Venetians, begging them to have pity on the Holy City and to help to redeem it from the infidels, began to seep away. But we are actually on the way! I bade my brave lady goodbye for who knows how many years!*

"She will rule well in my absence," the count continued. "You did not meet my only child, my Elizabeth. She is betrothed to a fine man who will become the count of St. Pol if I do not return."

William bent his head, not wanting to see the face of a man who so cheerfully went on Crusade

---
*Hugh of St. Pol died on the Crusade.

not knowing that he would ever return from it. Would he himself go if he felt it were his last time to look on his home and family? He shivered a little in the damp chill.

A few hours brought them to Béthune, where William found that the troubadour had already gone on. Everyone gladly hung his wet garments to steam where fires shut out the damp and made a bright background to talk.

"The first ships have left, William, and others are warping in to wharves for loading!" Tom almost had excitement in his voice.

They still had days to ride to port, and the boys' impatience, rain or not, made every delay tiresome. Had Simon gone on?

Hugh laughed at William's eager questions. "He finds much to do. Count Baldwin is glad to have him oversee the camp near the wharves and organize the knights. There is no one so proud and touchy as a poor knight with only his sword belt and spurs free of debt! It takes a diplomat with a heavy fist in reserve if needed to deal with them. Never fear being left behind. Our Simon does not forget his responsibilities. Even in the midst of quarrelsome subordinates. Tell me, do you and Tom ever disagree?"

"Tom does not say enough to disagree with," William laughed, "and I don't see the need of fighting with others. If I know those around me do not like my beliefs, I am learning to keep still. Tom is a good teacher."

At last Simon de Montfort, camped in a tent like the lowliest knight rather than sumptuously in one of Lord Baldwin's castles, saw the two boys approaching. Peter stayed by the horses.

"Aha! About time. I could have used a couple of pages with the ability to keep their eyes open and mouth shut. A messenger from Hugh told me you were almost here, so there are your pallets. Throw yourselves down for an hour until I have time to talk. Never mind your horses, I see servants coming to take care of them."

"I will help them." Tom turned back but stopped as Montfort wordlessly pointed at the bed on the floor.

"Lord Simon, we are three instead of two." William had no real anxiety about Peter's welcome. The lord remained silent, so he continued. "He is a retiring captain of my father's troops who chooses the Crusade rather than a cottage."

"An old soldier apt to command! We could use more like him. Will he be willing to be separated from you if needed on the horse transport? Our ship can convey only a few mounts."

Peter, waiting outside the tent flap, answered William's call. Simon at once approved of this survivor of forty years of campaigning. Although Peter stood respectfully, his posture indicated his experience and sense of his own worth. The baron lay back in his chair and smiled.

"Go to your bed, boy. Peter and I will talk."

William heard only the first low murmur and but dimly felt the thud as Tom followed literally Lord Simon's order to throw himself on the pallet. Gradually William lost the feeling of still swaying on horseback.

Although considered spacious, the command ship had room for only the leaders to have bunks to themselves. Those William and Tom used never had a chance to cool between shifts. If they wanted a nap, the two lads curled on top of casks of supplies, of which the deck contained many. Baldwin's plans did not depend on obtaining supplies from ports along the journey. Ships ahead of them, though, put in daily to the ports of the Spanish peninsula. Prices were high for the scanty supplies available there.

The ships dared not venture far from land. To the relief of Tom, the Bay of Biscay, notorious for storms, was good to them. Long swells rose and sank like the breathing of the sea. Except for the disturbing corkscrew motion as the ship hesitated at the crest of the swell before starting down the other side, none of the landsmen aboard had trouble.

The passengers entertained one another with storytelling sessions. Tales handed down from great-great- and even more-great-grandfathers kept the boys fascinated. At first, in sight of the white cliffs of England, they heard accounts of the Norman conquest. Next came yarns of the close link between Cornwall and Brittany, of one tongue on either side of the channel. Farther along they listened to the story of Roland and his knights. Still later the crew shared the exploits of the fishermen who sailed beyond the edge of the world—and returned with fish! Stories of the Moors in Spain predominated as they coasted along the Iberian shore. Those Spanish knights had no need to go to the Holy Land to face Saracens.

At the Spanish ports one would think he was even now in the Orient. The costumes were different and the customs strange. The boys longed to explore the narrow streets rising in steps from the harbors.

"I must suppose," Simon commented, "you would enjoy being carried off to be slaves in a Moorish household? William especially would bring a good price. They might make him a eunuch for the women's quarters. Now, Tom would probably go better as a galley slave. His muscles begin to bulge enough to catch a shipmaster's eye."

They gave up their thoughts of shore adventure.

Through the Pillars of Hercules the ships swept, one by one. The great Rock of Gibraltar surely constituted one of the pillars, but the other remained dim in the distance. Entry into the Mediterranean Sea gave rise to romantic fantasies, all of which Simon derided.

"We came at this time by intent," he stated prosaically. "If we meet at Venice by the end of June, we will reach our goal before winter sets in and the sea becomes dangerous."

Islands passed in far review. When they approached land for fresh water, the smiling inhabitants brought strange fruits that the Crusaders hauled aboard in bags from the low craft of the traders.

Malta—Melita of the Scriptures—inspired stories of Saint Paul, who had traveled those waters. The ships rounded the boot of Italy, and the long run up the Adriatic began. The days flowed into each other, wearing away at the nerves. One could not remain at the peak of excitement for so long. Though the boys looked constantly for Moslem pirates, the raiders of the haunted Mediterranean, they were not unhappy to be disappointed.

## Chapter Six

The winged lion of Saint Mark increasingly appeared on the sails of merchant ships. "That is the badge of Venice, lads," Montfort told them. "Note how they stay clear of us even when we carry the colors of Baldwin, and the white cross. The Venetians are shrewd traders. They dominate the north end of the Adriatic Sea and allow trade only through their own ports. The other cities of Italy are bitterly jealous and angry that we approached Venice for ships and supplies. But she is the great shipbuilding center. She boasts that she can construct and equip a war galley in one day!"

The boys longed to know how Peter did with the horses. They had only rarely caught a glimpse of the ships that carried the men-at-arms and their own mounts.

"I wouldn't even tease Peter about his ax if we could just see him," Tom confided. "He is a great old fellow."

"Why tease him at all?" William asked. "The English ax is a fine weapon for close work. King Richard prized it."

The boys fell thoughtful at that, remembering Richard of England, who had spent so little time in his homeland. His lion heart had not been of great value to England, and now his brother—best not even think criticism of him. King John had "long ears."

A vessel neared them with the winged lion displayed. On the prow stood a man who evidently meant to hail them. He wore the red of a magistrate of Venice.

"I believe we are being officially welcomed." Count Baldwin came from his deck pavilion along with Conan of Béthune, known to the Venetians as one of the six ambassadors of the year before, who spoke for the count. The Venetian ship turned to lead them to their assigned port, its long sweeps* swirling the water.

Conan leaned on the railing. "San Nicolo is to be our base. It is an island especially equipped to house knights and men, and our people should be comfortable. Baldwin, will you camp with your men or accept the hospitality of the doge?"†

My place is with my barons and knights," the count stated, "but I suppose I must accept entertainment from the doge, Henry Dandolo."

The great count of Flanders, second only to Boniface, marquis of Montferrat, who had been elected supreme leader of the Crusade, knew he must receive special honors. He looked to Montfort.

"I will make the troops my business," Simon assured his lord.

"Hold yourself in readiness in case I need you, and these two young squires of yours."

The color rose in William's cheeks at being singled out. He had not known that Baldwin had so much as noticed him.

"Lads," the count advised, "learn the Venetian tone. Talk with them. Make friends. Keep your ears

---
*sweeps: long oars
†doge: the governor of Venice

open. You never know what you might learn."

William answered in the few words he already knew of the Venetian language. Ship travel offered plenty of free time, but learning a new language came less easily to him than to Tom. Baldwin laughed and clapped his shoulder.

San Nicolo held better accommodations than they had expected, with room for thirty thousand Crusaders, horse and man. Ferries daily brought fresh water, food, and fodder.

"Our poor horses!" the boys exclaimed when the animals at last arrived. The shadow-thin remnants of their once sturdy mounts grieved them. "Couldn't we take them to the mainland for grazing?"

"This couldn't be helped, lads," Peter consoled them. "They do not like sea travel. But they will soon pick up, with their feet on solid ground, and will get stronger with exercise. I wish we could have green pasture, though."

Crusaders straggled in a few boatloads at a time. The expedition leaders had set June 29 as the day to sail so as to take advantage of summer weather. Yet less than a third of the expected number of knights had arrived by that time. Montfort looked worried.

"Some of them have gone to other ports, to make their own way to Palestine. That upsets all the original plans and shorts us of money. They do not trust the Venetians." And in a lower voice, "Neither do I."

He spoke these words in the presence of the boys alone. They stood at a sea wall, watching supplies unloaded, seeing the sullen expressions of the sailors, hearing the angry tones of the French representatives. One of the latter called to Montfort, "They have doubled the price on us—again!"

"What is this?" Simon demanded. "Venice made a bargain with us to supply us for nine months, beginning the twenty-ninth."

"We haven't seen the color of your money," growled the captain. "I don't get paid by the doge until you pay him, so I have to charge you directly." He spat in the water. "It looks as though you're trying to cheat us. Where are the thirty thousand who were to have been here?"

"On the way," Simon answered, his voice in tight control. "Unload your vessel, then take me to St. Marks."

The boys accompanied him to the palace of the doge, the great Venetian ruler. William had seen him only at a distance, his aged figure still erect, and his almost sightless eyes seeming to penetrate the very thoughts of those with whom he consulted. Baldwin, Conan, Geoffroy de Villehardouin, and others of the Crusader leaders had already gathered there, waiting to see the doge.

"Wait for us outside," Simon said to the lads. "Wander and listen."

"We will keep our ears open," William replied.

The Venetians' arrogance made listening easy. The citizens seemed not to know or care that the two might overhear their comments. Constantly the Venetians expressed contempt for the Crusaders.

The square of St. Mark's, partially surrounded

by open-air shops and vendors, had seen Conan, Geoffroy, and the four other envoys lying on their faces, weeping and begging for help to free Jerusalem. Ten thousand Venetians had shouted agreement, but apparently only if they were paid. The debasement of the French knights apparently left a lasting impression on the Venetian mind.

Tom expressed William's thoughts as the two looked around the square, on which the palace fronted, as well as the church of St. Mark. "Look at them, selling trinkets and food on the steps of their church. Venetians are all shopkeepers, from the least to the greatest. They grab for profit, which is more important to them than freeing the Holy City."

Footsteps pounded through the crowd, and an excited boy burst into view. "Frenchmen! Frenchmen! Someone comes from the Alps!"

Forgetting their orders to stay in the square, Tom and William followed their guide at the same dead run. A person could not go far without coming to water in this city of islands. Even before they reached the canal, they saw the traveler from the Alps. Gaunt and clothed in rags, he was a pitiful sight. The boatman who brought him held him fast by the arm, which was just as well. The fellow would have fallen without support. The Venetian shook him. "You said someone would pay me!"

Tom grasped the stranger and sat him on a stone set upright for mooring boats, while William exploded, "Here!" He tossed a silver denarius to the angry boatman. In the wayfarer's garments he recognized the stout raiment with which Fulk of

Neuilly had clothed his Crusaders. The white cross was almost invisible.

Tom and William's guide danced excitedly around them, saying, "I did it. I led you to him, young sirs!" while a wide ring of urchins jeered at him.

With a nod William gave the lad a silver penny, rich pay for the deed. The other boys shut up, while the young guide mocked at them in turn. The whole group wandered off, demanding to know how the suddenly wealthy one would spend it.

"It is all right, you are safe now. We are of Lord Montfort and Count Baldwin."

The man nodded his shaggy head and started to weep, great tears running down his unshaven cheeks. Unshaven for weeks, though it was not at all the custom in France. He tried again and again to speak, choked, laid his head against William, and succumbed to what the boys recognized as immense grief, as well as the result of exhaustion and starvation.

A bell jangled, and Tom saw a band of milk goats approaching the landing, where a flatboat was obviously theirs from the evidence left in it. The owner, a cheerful, blocky young woman, stopped to stare at the trio.

"Milk?" she said hopefully. "I can drain a little more from these pets of mine."

William eagerly agreed. Shortly they held a bowl to the lips of the forlorn Crusader. A few sips exhausted him. After several catches of breath he finally swallowed it all. The goat maid watched sympathetically. William held out some money.

"No, no. This is given for the sake of the Christ." Her charges were already aboard, and she shoved off, waving to them before poling away.

"I take back what I said about *all* Venetians," Tom growled.

The survivor grew calmer now and looked up with eyes still wet. "Father Fulk is dead."

His statement stunned the boys. "I feel like crying too," William said glumly. "When did it happen?"

"A month ago, before we were well into the Alps. A wasting sickness. He still tried to say Jerusalem with his last breath."

Tom swallowed hard, his dark face immobile. "What of the others? Many thousands were coming."

The old man struggled to speak. (Old? William wondered.) "They were too many for the land to feed. Fulk had money, but what good is it when there is naught to buy? The peasants hid what little they had left. Only the first of those following the cross had any strength left when the time came to go over the high passes. I am one of those."

With a horrible laugh he showed his wasted arm. "I don't think one in ten will get here."

"Tom," William ordered, "run to Lord Montfort with the news, and get help on the way. I will take care of him."

As the squire started off, William bent toward the soldier. "What is your name?"

"Wulf. Wulf of Eu."

"Then you know me?"

The Crusader wearily nodded. "The English

boy, brother of the young lord who is the betrothed of our maid of Eu." A heavy sob shook him.

Patiently William waited for him to stop. A peasant poled to the landing with a load of fresh vegetables, which gave the lad a thought. "Friend, could you tell us of a place on the mainland where we could find pasture for a few horses?"

The farmer leaned on his pole and slowly assessed the two figures, the boy, well dressed, evidently well off, supporting the starved, ragged man. Obviously he made up his mind slowly. "How many?" he asked at last.

"Five or six."

"You will have to send men to guard them from raiders. I don't keep animals myself because of the thieves from the hills, but there is pasture too wet to plant. A shed too to shelter the guards. It needs fixing." He stopped to tie up the boat before finishing. "They must feed themselves. My woman won't cook for them."

"Good enough." William paused to note the position of the sun. "Will you be here at Angelus?"*

The peasant nodded and strode off with a shoulder yoke supporting two enormous sacks of vegetables.

Wulf glanced up. "I could help guard the horses, young sir."

"Can you walk now?" William asked. "We will go slowly to the square."

The pent-up horror seemed to burst in Wulf, and he would not stop talking. At times he ran out

---

*Angelus: a prayer (in this case, said at noon)

of breath so badly they had to rest for a few moments.

"The great birds!* They seemed big enough to carry off a man!" He shuddered. "One of them dropped a bone on the rocks and shattered it. It was a thigh bone, a human bone!" He paused to catch his breath. "I know the bone of a man when I see it." he challenged the boy, who had not said a word. "It could have been one of the Crusaders!

"Fulk promised that if we died on Crusade we would go directly to heaven. God is having a hard time finding places for all the new ones." The Crusader paused for a few tears. "I don't mean that disrespectfully, you understand. Why didn't He provide manna for us, or quails, or something? Fulk thought God would. We were going on His behalf."

Having had a little nourishment, Wulf walked more strongly now. William stopped to buy bread from a vendor and tore it into pieces. Wulf crammed chunks into his mouth so fast the English boy would not give him much at a time.

"I asked for food at villages along the way, on this side of the Alps," the Crusader said when he finished eating. "They were more likely to set the dogs on me than throw me a crust of bread."

They reached the square to find Tom on the point of embarking for San Nicolo with a message. William hurried Wulf to him. "Tell Peter I have found pasture for a few horses, six at least, but they will have to be guarded. I meet the farmer at

---

*lammergeiers: vultures that live on bone marrow

the hour of Angelus."

"The leaders still have not been able to meet the doge and his council," Tom stated angrily. "I will take Wulf. You go to Lord Montfort and see which of his horses he will risk at pasture."

At the palace, the impatient knight's strove to control their anger at being kept so long stewing in their uncertainty. "He does this on purpose to arouse our ire," Montfort informed William calmly. "Wrathful adversaries are easier to handle. Look at Count Baldwin, however. Instead of responding in anger, he is enjoying a pleasant social hour. Well done of Baldwin, I say."

The English lad told him of the possible pasture, and the baron answered, "Very well. Meet the farmer, learn his terms, and if he will supply transport. Then report back."

The terms were high, as expected, but Montfort gladly accepted them. "At least two good things have occurred today, though not an interview with the doge. We return tomorrow for that. Other business took too long today."

News of the mountain catastrophe cast a pall of gloom among the barons. Many had taken the cross at the hand of Fulk, and they grieved deeply for him. Several parties set out by different routes to find and relieve the remnants of the vast army of peasants who had tried to reach Venice by land.

# Chapter Seven

Montfort shook his head. "The Crusaders are gathering so slowly! It is July, and Montferrat, our leader, is not here yet. I fear we have only a third of the number our envoys bargained transport and supplies to sustain. They planned on 30,000 men and horses for 4,500 knights."

William wore an anxious expression much of the time, for his lord's burdens rested heavily on his young shoulders. He felt the band around his waist, a gesture which became habitual.

Tom nudged him once when he saw him doing it. "Don't you dare! Your grandmother gave you your few gold bezants for extreme emergency only. This is not yet as bad as it will be. Your money would not feed twelve thousand."

Shouts and voices caught their attention. Geoffroy de Villehardouin led his horse and a contingent of others, all knights with horses. Tom darted off to hear the news.

"Geoffroy's master, the count of Blois, is at Pavia and seems to have decided to go to another port," he reported in a few minutes. "Geoffroy signed the agreement with Venice in his lord's name, and if Blois does not honor it——! No wonder Geoffroy is in a hurry."

Most of the horses did not look good. Montfort agreed with the boys that their own mounts were in better shape on the marshy pasture. It kept them healthier and stronger than a dry stall with limited amounts of water and feed would have. Since new provisions no longer arrived every day at San Nicolo, the Crusaders tightened their belts.

"The doge pushes us toward something other than what we planned," Montfort told Baldwin. "Many of the knights cannot see why the leaders want to attack Melik, Saladin's brother, in Egypt. They do not realize that the heart of the Saracen Empire lies in Egypt. If the heart is pierced, it accomplishes more than chopping off the extremities. And the Venetian fleet sits waiting while we try to find the eighty-five thousand marks we agreed to pay."

William whistled under his breath. "I have never seen even *one* mark!"

"And you won't!" Montfort's face lightened. "It is money of exchange, not money in the hand, like bezants. You lads get used to eating from wooden platters. My silver dishes go to the money lenders to collect a few more marks."

The English page's hand went again to the belt beneath his tunic. Tom warned him again with a glance.

"We could hire a boat and go after supplies," Tom suggested to the baron.

"With the Venetian fleet watching every move?" Montfort snorted. "The doge wants us hungry enough to do anything he dictates."

The troubadours kept a continuing contest under way among the Crusaders. Nowhere else in the world could the lads have heard such fine music. Conan of Béthune they already revered for his marvelous playing and singing. Now they learned to know Guy of Coucy, another baron whose love was more for his lute than for his sword. Even so he taught the boys new tricks with the sword in their daily drill.

"Wait until Renaud arrives! When Boniface of Montferrat comes with his troops, we will start all over." Conan's north French accent now seemed commonplace to the boys. When singers from the south made fun of it and imitated Picardy accent and ways, it irritated Tom and William. However, no one made light of his singing.

"Ah, love, how hard it is to leave thee!" The sighing of the troubadours found an echo in most hearts. Always, before the gathering broke up, someone asked for one of the great Crusader hymns.

> "They stand, those walls of Zion,
>    All jubilant with song
> And bright with many an angel
>    And all the martyr throng.
>
> "The Prince is ever in them,
>    The daylight is serene.
> The pastures of the blessed
>    Are decked with glorious sheen.
>
> "O sweet and blessed country,
>    The home of God's elect,
> O sweet and blessed country
>    That eager hearts expect.
>
> "Jesus, in mercy bring us
>    To that dear land of rest,

Who art, with God the Father
And Spirit, ever blessed."

Tom, seeing the wide-eyed rapturous look on his young lord's face, gave him an impatient shake. "That song tells of the heavenly Jerusalem, not the one on earth. If you saw the earthly one, you'd find it full of beggars, sick people, and dirt, like any other city."

"I know it," William replied without resentment. "It *ought* to be like that hymn, anyway."

"A lot more Crusaders will get to the heavenly Jerusalem than the earthly one, the way things are going," his squire replied.

"Right." William remembered the multiplied thousands dead on the trails through the mountains, and the painfully few their rescue parties found and brought in. Bad as he had looked, Wulf had been one of the strongest.

The boys begged permission to stay with the horse guards at the pasture. Montfort looked sharply at them, then decided that better eating and abundant water proved motive enough, and let them go.

Peter and Wulf looked fat and amazingly relaxed compared with their rationed companions on San Nicolo. The boys' escort from the island left after enjoying a full meal, and carried back as much as they could without arousing the attention of the Venetians.

"What mischief are you two planning?" Peter asked with a twinkle after the others left.

Tom gave an unaccustomed grin. "You don't

know how bad it is on San Nicolo. We told a couple of closemouthed friends to be at a darkened stretch of beach at one o'clock every night (not midnight——people are suspicious of midnight!) and they might find a surprise."

"No need of guards here if the horses are on the trail, loaded with waterskins and meal," Peter said. "We will all be in on the surprise."

Dried fruits, smoked meat, and anything else they could acquire by scattering out and buying in quantities kept them busy during the day.

"But what are six loads—all we can carry with our horses— going to do among the thousands on the island?" William asked. The small amount tended to depress him.

"The Venetians supply enough to keep them living, barely," Tom replied. "This is extra. It will count."

The local populace felt indulgent toward the hungry, sleepy boys. Everyone knew how much growing boys ate. William's fairness and seeming fragility especially helped overcome suspicion and reluctance. Tom grew popular for his watchcare of his young lord.

Montfort summoned the boys to meet him at St. Mark's Square. "I am puzzled," he began. "We used to have some jealousy and claims of favoritism. Now I hear nothing but good of you, with no reason for the change."

Tom gave a slight shrug. William looked surprised and thoughtful. "I try always to be courteous to my elders, whatever their rank, and ——"

A snort from a member of the escort turned into

a cough and an apologetic look. Montfort again faced the boys, his mouth in a grim line. "I suspect every man-at-arms on San Nicolo knows something I do not. I am thinking of recalling you."

He got a reaction from that. "My lord, do we have to go back to the island?" William wailed. Even Tom looked alarmed.

The escort who had coughed said carefully, "I hear they eat a great deal. Probably they are growing so fast they find our short rations more painful than grown men."

Gratefully William received the suggestion, then noticed the smile lurking behind Simon's sternness. He decided his lord knew more than he and Tom had thought.

"You may go back with the horse guard, but *be careful.* The count of Blois is almost here, adding to our number, and even two less on San Nicolo helps."

"Lord Simon, how go the discussions with the doge?"

They noticed a touch of gray at Montfort's temples. All the leaders seemed to have aged in the past month.

"They do not go. Dandolo insists on the full sum, eighty-five thousand marks, before we depart, but we simply do not have it. So far we have only one third of the men the envoys expected, yet he holds us to the full amount. I cannot think what that scheming mind has in its depths. His religion is his city's welfare, and he plans something to the advantage of Venice. He cares nothing for Jerusalem in the hands of Saracens."

Simon talked more to himself than to the boys. He sighed heavily as he started toward the palace and the endless waiting.

In a window above, the boys saw framed a lad younger than themselves who looked into the patio and the sunshine with longing eyes. When he noticed Tom and William staring, he backed away as if he wished not to be seen. His behaviour attracted their curiosity.

"I wish," William said thoughtfully as they walked to their boat, "that Boniface of Montferrat would come. He is the elected leader. Perhaps he will bring enough money to make up the amount."

"Now, Willie," Tom replied, "you know those who have the least distance to travel are always the last to arrive. And he is not the only one missing. Some never started. Others went to other ports in spite of their pledges, not trusting the Venetians. I think the chief trouble is that the Crusade has been too long building. If it could have embarked even one year after the great tournament when the most lords took the cross, all that enthusiasm would not have seeped away."

William drew a deep breath. "Sometimes"—he spoke softly as if afraid he might be overheard—"I wonder if maybe Wulf was right. God did not do miracles for the people coming afoot because He knew this crusade is useless."

"Hush, Willie." His squire glanced uneasily around. "You know that the Holy Father in Rome has promoted this as the high point of his career. Surely he of all men would know what our Lord wants. Pope Innocent has even taxed the monasteries and convents to help pay for outfitting the poor. He must be finding all this waiting as aggravating as we do."

Tom looked critically at his master. "Look at you! You are growing fast. Already your wrists stick out of your sleeves, and your hosen are worn out. I think we must get out one of those bezants for new clothes."

Indeed William had grown taller. He overtopped Tom, though his shoulders were not so broad. However, they still had more width than of old, and strained at his armor links.

"You cannot use a sword easily with the armor binding you," Tom observed. "Let us go to San Nicolo and find the armorer, to enlarge it."

The boys came and went as they pleased now, for the Venetians could see no harm in the sleepy-eyed awkwardness of William and his companion. Other than them, only official parties left the island. The men-at-arms grumbled much from idleness and lack of exercise, in spite of constant competition in war skills.

"Swim. You will never have a better chance," William suggested to the men. He and Tom demonstrated. "We Wye men learned in colder water than this."

"We Wye men!" mocked one genially. "They washed me when I was born and they can wash me when I die. That is enough!"

William continued to grow taller and thinner. The tailor made tucks in his sleeves. They would soon need to be let out. The lad also grew sleepier. Brief naps could not make up for nights of leading the horses by devious ways to the water's edge and rowing strenuously to reach the island. He would return with emptied waterskins and sacks, riding to the pasture before daylight. Moonlit nights offered needed breaks, however. Then the boys could sleep long hours, visit St. Mark's Square, and practice their swordsmanship.

"You are thinner than we are!" Montfort commented curiously. "Where do you put all that food we hear about?"

# Chapter Eight

August. The Crusaders had been waiting more than two months on San Nicolo. The boys now stood against the wall behind Simon de Montfort, watching the leaders confer among themselves. At last they had their official expedition head—for all the good that did, William thought to himself.

Boniface, marquis of Montferrat, had a special interest in the Holy Land. His elder brother, Conrad, made king of Jerusalem by King Richard, had promptly been assassinated. Had Boniface a desire to replace Amaury of Lusignan, who ruled in exile on Cyprus? A closemouthed fellow, this Boniface.

"Has each of you put all his silver serving vessels into the cause?" the marquis asked. "I also will use mine for the purpose. Will it be enough?"

Baldwin doubtfully shook his head. Louis of Blois looked downhearted. (Probably wishing he had gone on to Pisa, William assumed.) St. Pol waited for the others to speak, and when none did, he explained, "There are so many poor knights who cannot pay their fare. Some who have paid are restless and disgruntled. They wish either to go on at once or be freed to go home. We can hardly blame them."

"I can!" Geoffroy snorted. As one of the original envoys to Venice, perhaps he realized that part of the problem existed because of an earlier overenthusiastic estimate of the number of Crusaders. "When they took the cross they pledged their lives, weal or woe. Hardship is no excuse for crawling home like curs."

Montfort attempted to head off what could become an open quarrel. "How much will we have, including that of my lord marquis?"

Baldwin found a paper much written upon and overmarked. "No matter how you add it, it comes out the same—fifty-two thousand marks. We are short by thirty-three thousand."

"Let us talk to Doge Dandolo again and try to get some concession." Boniface looked more hopeful than the others. He had not their experience with the Venetian ruler.

"That old man is like flint. I mean, hard!" Blois stated. "We have to tell him this is the last and best we can do. Conditions are bad among the men. Some of the troops recently killed and ate one of their precious horses!"

A long silence followed. It did not raise their spirits that Boniface would speak for them. They had passed almost beyond hope.

And, William realized, that was just where Dandolo and his purple-robed council wanted them. "I wonder what he will offer?" the boy whispered to Tom. "When he is so able at 95 years, what was he at 40?"

William's merry voice startled the gloom as he answered his own question: "Learning all the cunning he uses now!" No one frowned at him, and the group relaxed a bit.

"Perhaps William is cheerful because he is not confined to San Nicolo," Geoffroy suggested.

Montfort shook his head. "Of us all, these lads

are the only ones doing something that helps. It does lift the spirits. I wish a few more could do likewise. What they bring is only a drop among so many, but it cheers the men immensely."

Dandolo promised Boniface that he would try to influence his council and the larger administrative body below them. Possibly they could work something out. Finally the doge summoned the Crusade leaders, the first time it had happened without their request. A tiny flame of hope raced through San Nicolo. A breakthrough?

Coming out of the palace, Baldwin, Louis, Boniface, and the others halted on the steps. They looked at one another with dazed expressions.

"How can we do what he suggests?" Montfort demanded. "We are pledged to fight Saracens, not Christians!"

The count of Blois swung his head like a sick bull. "Can we delay or bargain further? A few more months and our money will be used up for nothing and we will be stranded helpless."

He had not waited as long as Baldwin and the contingent from northern France. Tom and William drifted closer, wondering what proposition the doge had offered.

"Come," Baldwin commanded. "This is not for public discussion." He looked severely at the boys.

Montfort gave a wintry smile. "I doubt if others are as closemouthed as these lads, Baldwin." Then he whispered, "They are my eyes and ears, not my voice."

The great count of Flanders sharply eyed William's innocent, youthful expression and had to smile. "Where would indiscretion place your patron, lads?"

As usual, Tom's face did not change, but his young master portrayed grief, pain, and reproach. "Sire! My lord!"

Simon waved the lad's reaction aside. "Never mind. I want to know what you hear in the streets."

They perched at the prow of the boat that conveyed them to the prison island. Only Balwin and Montfort heard.

"The name, Zara. It is a city on the eastern shore of the Adriatic, in Dalmatia. The Venetians are angry because Zara cuts into their trade. Venice wants all trading done here for the whole Adriatic Sea. All foreigners must stop here to buy, and the other cities must come here for exchange, so Venice charges them both coming and going. Zara is not pledged to Venice but to Hungary. The king of Hungary wrested it from Venice. Her trade originates from the East—very rich—and she extends welcome to all trading ships. The Venetians are losing money they feel is theirs."

"That explains it," Baldwin interjected. "Money, always money to the Venetians. Thank you, lads."

Montfort talked to the boys. "The doge says he will accept the fifty-two thousand marks and delay asking for the remainder—if we will join Venice in the capture of Zara, making it subject to Venice and her laws. The spoils of the city should bring enough to pay the remaining thirty-three thousand marks."

The boys remained silent until they landed and walked to the council chamber. "Do you remember the oath Humphrey swore at his knighting?" William asked, controlling his tears.

"Yes," Tom answered shortly. "I took it also, in my heart. To help the helpless, using his sword only for good and noble deeds. All these great lords and knights swore the same thing. Now Doge Dandolo demands that they do just the opposite."

"I wonder what our Lord Christ thinks of this!" his young master burst out.

The leaders seemed short of words. "My men are hungry and thirsty," St. Pol doggedly repeated. Seeing William's flush, he barked, "Do not take my words to yourself, boy. I am only at my wits' end."

So also with the others. They found themselves forced into a corner with no way out save at the word of the doge. The wily Venetian waited for their answer. It was obvious to most that there could be only one.

Food and water appeared in abundance immediately upon the signing of the new contract. The men-at-arms lost their apathy and began shining their arms and practicing with new fervor.

"Does the Holy Father know what is happening to his Crusade?" William muttered to his companion.

"He will find out," Tom grunted. He looked less drawn now that the nightly expeditions had ended. Even William's bones began to have better covering, and the hollows behind his jaws to fill in. At least some good came of the agreement.

The secret did not get out, though rumors sped through the camp. "It is too late to sail for Palestine," some commented. "Something else is up." Fantastic tales spread.

Henry Dandolo called for a great gathering in St. Mark's Square. The doge himself ascended the pulpit. His address praised the Crusaders for their high and holy enterprise, for the attempt to free Jerusalem. In spite of their knowledge of the doge's scheme, his speech provoked tears among the Crusade leaders, as well as his own people. The noble expression of the almost blind old leader captivated them.

He threw out his arms in an ecstasy of approval as he said, "What can I do, old and feeble as I am? I can but join these noble cavaliers in their holy enterprise! Let my son, Rainer, take the rule in Venice. I will live or die with the pilgrims of the cross!"

On his knees before the altar, he affixed the white cross to his high cotton cap. The people and many of the Crusaders wept.

But he carefully arranged that Venice must share the profits of any conquests the expedition made.

Early October found the fleet loading. It included 50 fighting galleys, 240 troopships, 70 supply vessels, and 120 flat-bottomed palanders for the horses.

"An envoy has come from Pope Innocent," Tom murmured to Montfort. "The doge will not let him talk to the French."

Simon had already determined not to take part in warfare against Christians, so he went to Boniface with the news of the envoy's arrival.

The Crusade leader returned from the doge. "He

refuses to allow the envoy, Peter Capuano, to accompany us as the emissary of the pope. If he comes, it is to be solely as a preacher. Peter has already started for Rome to report."

Loading completed, the majestic fleet swept away from Venice, Dandolo leading from a high platform in the prow of the first vessel. But they would not head directly for Zara. Instead they would visit all the cities around the northern Adriatic for processions, great church services, and most important—the boys believed—to demonstrate the power of Venice. The king of Hungary, who ruled inland, must be awed into leaving Venice in possession of reconquered Zara.

With favoring winds, it required only one day to reach Zara from Venice. In poor weather six days would do it. The Crusader fleet took six weeks, displaying their might along the coast.

Boniface remained in Venice. Sick? Waiting for couriers from home? Or nervous? The boys could only speculate.

# Chapter Nine

On November 10 the great fleet sailed into the harbor at Zara. The city walls were high and strong, the gates firmly closed, flanked by towers to protect them.

"It is not a large city," William remarked. "Our army must have three times as many as the whole population. Even with such splendid walls they could not hold out long."

"Especially since the Venetians provided scores of siege machines, catapults, mangonels,* and such." Tom's gloom deepened. "Look at our Lord Simon. He has been getting more and more rebellious at the thought of attacking this city."

Dandolo and his ship swung close to the frowning walls. The boys could see his scarlet robe and the high cap with the white cross. No wonder Simon cringed at the contrast between professed piety and the actions of the doge. From their own ship the northern Frenchmen and Baldwin's Flemish listened as the Venetian called out in an amazingly strong voice, "Surrender yourselves and your city to Venice, your rightful rulers. Give up your rebelliousness and live!"

"Watch Simon!" William muttered.

The baron ceased his pacing and sprang to a rail as close as he could get to the blank, silent walls. "Defy him, you citizens of Zara! He has no right to attack you!"

---
*mangonels: devices for hurling missiles

For a moment a stunned silence fell over the fleet, followed by cries of outrage from the watching crews of the ships of Venice.

"Well, Simon," Baldwin drawled, "you have set the cat among the pigeons for certain. If there had been a chance of immediate surrender, they will not do it now, thinking a division exists among us."

"I will have no part in a siege of this Christian city," Montfort snarled.

"Then you must take your men and camp well away from the rest of the army. See, they are landing already. What a grim array the knights make with their featureless cylindrical casques."*

From landing so frequently for exercise, the sturdy, blocky horses had remained in good condition. The knights led the men-at-arms to surround the landward side of the little city. The Venetians held the seaward side with their ships.

After Baldwin disembarked, Montfort's men came to shore. One look at the baron's grim face discouraged any opposition. Simon's men loaded camping equipment and his pavilion on horses and turned along the coast north some miles to set up their own little village.

"I'm glad Simon pulled out of that mess," William whispered to his partner. Tom nodded.

Daily Montfort and a company of his own rode to a hill overlooking the besieged city. The great camp of the Crusaders surrounded it, the colorful pavilions of the barons making the city outside the gray walls look more alive than the drab interior.

---
*casques: helmets

The Crusaders made no attempt to assault the gates. They trundled giant siege machines into place and anchored them. Heavy stones arched into the city or crashed against the walls. Elsewhere, "mice" burrowed, the miners digging at the foundations being protected by overhead shields.

A commotion among the leaders attracted Montfort's attention, and with a select party he paced his steed to the meeting. "See the colors and badges. It is another envoy from Pope Innocent," he told his page.

The abbot, another Peter, announced the message. "If you attack a Christian city—and His Holiness specifies Zara!—you will be excommunicated!"

While the abbott surveyed the machines being wound to deliver another barrage of stones, the French leaders glanced at one another, carefully avoiding Montfort's mocking gaze.

Excommunication! The worst threat to any Western Christian. No weddings, no funeral services, no baptisms or christenings, the church doors locked, and no priestly functions at all. Those men winding the catapults would take it seriously even if the leaders didn't. Baldwin and his peers politely led Abbot Peter to a comfortable pavilion and as politely refused to allow him to leave or to talk to their men. The siege went on.

A wall began to crumble, and a great shout went up. Not the catapults and the mangonels, but the "mice" gnawing away below had prevailed.

A white flag appeared above the main gate. The laboring soldiers at the machines rested on their levers, and a long wait followed. The knights sat still as statues, their lances at rest pointing skyward. The ponderous gates could not move until the guards had pounded away the bars and blocks. Then they swung slowly open.

On foot the city council came forth, led by their mayor. Dressed in their best, they came prepared for death or what penalties the victors might lay on them. They were not soldiers, only merchants who had dared to defy Venice.

Montfort's men silently stood or sat on the hill watching the procession from the city advance with bowed heads and funeral tread.

"They have lost everything," William mourned, "perhaps even life itself. For Venice to grow richer!"

After one savage shout as the gates opened, the massive army remained still. The men from Zara knelt before the ranks of knights and barons, in complete submission.

"I do not believe," Montfort stated slowly, "that lives will be demanded. Venice wants more trade, not to destroy what already exists. They will lose all their goods, however."

So it proved. The Crusaders and the Venetians agreed on equal shares of the loot. No door could be locked against them, and the invaders raided every house, carrying everything of value to a great heap, where they divided it. Silent householders must stand aside and watch while the invaders carried their possessions away.

For the savage era in which they lived, it was a gentle victory. No burning and slaying occurred. The leaders scrupulously observed the rules they set. Still King Emeric of Hungary lost a city and raged over his loss at the hands of fellow Crusaders, fellow wearers of the white cross.

Fall storms prevented any further advance toward their Palestine goal. At this season the sea made a perilous "moat." The conquerors moved into Zara, requisitioning any houses they chose. Montfort also had to find quarters in the city. The Venetians took the part closest to the waterfront and their vessels, while the French held the rest of Zara. The lately arrived German knights shared the French portion. The Germans and their knightly priests to a man denounced the capture of the city, but they too were dependent on the Venetians.

Many of the lesser knights and men-at-arms showed their contempt for those from Venice. Fighting between the Crusaders and the Venetians broke out again and again. It took great tact and diplomacy by the leaders to avert full-scale war

"Do not go on the streets alone," Montfort warned the boys. But they grew bored with confinement.

"Marquis Montferrat is here with a surprise for us," the word spread among the Crusaders one day. "Come."

Finally their elected leader had arrived. By now it was the middle of December. With him, dressed in Oriental splendor—"the boy we saw at the window of the doge's palace!" William pressed closer to Simon to give him the information.

Montfort nodded. "He is said to have arrived only recently from Constantinople, where his uncle had imprisoned him. His father, Isaac Angelus, was deposed and blinded by his own brother. This is Alexius IV, the prince of Constantinople. Hush and listen."

The scarlet-robed doge, supported by the purple of the council and the red of the magistrates, made an imposing display. Boniface of Montferrat ceremoniously introduced young Alexius. The prince went on his knees to beg pity and support for himself and his blinded father, the rightful rulers of the Eastern empire.

The impressive show swayed the Crusaders.

"The liars!" Tom growled. "He was in the doge's palace all summer."

The remark shocked the spectators near the dark boy. They could see for themselves that the youth and the ancient Venetian met now for the first time.

Alexius explained that he first went to the pope, who refused to help him because Innocent was in the process of negotiating with the actual ruler of the empire. The boy said he then journeyed to territory belonging to Philip of Swabia, the husband of his sister, which explained how he came to be in the company of the marquis of Montferrat. Philip was overlord of some of Montferrat's lands.

William gasped. "I was positive Boniface hid something. He knew of this all the time."

"Have pity on a homeless, helpless boy!" Alexius continued. "Help to regain the throne for my father, who was blinded by that monster of cruelty, his own brother!" The prince's face flushed with zeal. "I promise, I promise! I will take the cross myself once Constantinople is regained. With ten thousand men provisioned for a year. I promise two hundred thousand silver marks to the Crusade. I promise five hundred knights to the continual support of Jerusalem."

His statements stirred both the cupidity of the Venetians and the chivalric ardor of the Crusaders.

"Constantinople is practically on our way," some proclaimed, showing their vague ideas of geography. "It would not be against our vows to succor the helpless."

The clergy found themselves divided over the request. For three hundred years the church had been splitting into East and West. The Eastern Church had rejected the sovereignty of Rome, so some priests thought it not wrong to attack the city of Constantinople. "It is not like the Zarans, who belong to our own church."

A letter soon arrived from Pope Innocent, who furiously denounced the capture of Zara. His own spies had taken him word.

"The Holy Father excommunicates the Crusaders over this," the boys discussed among themselves. "What will he say of Constantinople?"

Captain Peter and Wulf listened, and Peter shuddered. "It won't bother the Venetians who put them up to it. Their god is money!

"Many French knights want to go home and are slipping away one by one with their few followers," Peter commented. "Venice will not take them, so they are trying it by land."

"Not many will succeed alive, with such a small force to command respect," Wulf replied. "What thinks Montfort?"

William shook his head. "He talked to Baldwin. The count of Flanders has already signed the commitment to go to Constantinople. Simon will not. How can all this be pleasing to God? I wish we could go on to Palestine."

"It is pleasing to the Venetians! They are particularly angry at the Eastern empire because Alexius' uncle refused to continue a trade compact with Venice and has given it to Pisa, Venice's greatest rival."

"The wealthiest trade in the world," William agreed. "You can see why Venice wants this war."

Tom shrugged. "I hear Lord Simon returning. Let me see what he has found out."

Montfort wore a face like a thundercloud. He stalked past the boys and sank into a chair, resting his chin on his fist, elbow supported by the table. The boys remained still. It was not a time for questions. After a long silence, Simon drew a deep breath and looked up at the lads.

"Baldwin has signed for Constantinople. Montferrat has signed. Long ago the Eastern empire gave the Montferrats the kingdom of Thessalonica, but his family never claimed it. Now he wants it. That is his price for aiding Venice." Contempt colored the baron's tone. "St. Pol signed. Blois signed."

The boys waited. Finally Simon continued. "I have formally broken my covenant with Baldwin. What do you wish to do, lads? You may make a choice. He will accept you."

Silently William knelt before Montfort, his hands together in prayer position, for renewal of his pledge to Montfort. The baron gave a snort of laughter as Tom joined his young master.

"You do not know where I might go! Therefore I'll tell you so you may change your mind if you wish. I have sent an emissary to King Emeric of Hungary asking permission to cross his territory on the way by land around the northern end of the Adriatic Sea, to find another way to Palestine."

They held their hands up to be enclosed in his.

## Chapter Ten

*O*ther barons and knights would join Simon for his land adventure. It made quite a little army of their own. The Crusaders who signed for Constantinople became bitter about their leaving. However, the two young companions did not allow it to disturb them.

Enguerrand of Troyes, second in command to Montfort, lived a few houses down the steep cobbled street in Zara. At almost dusk a rider clattered through the city gate just before it closed for the night, and demanded the ear of Montfort.

"Aha!" Simon shouted, springing to his feet. "An answer from King Emeric. He knows we had nothing to do with the siege of Zara and offers us any help we need. He even sends a detachment of his own to escort us so we will have no problems with his people. Here, take this to Enguerrand."

Little traffic filled the streets at that hour. The natives of Zara kept themselves inconspicuous at all times. The French were at their evening meal, their prayers, or their drinking and singing. Tom and William plunged into the street and proceeded at a jog. Enough light still illumined the street to show their overtunic colors and the swords bumping their legs. Baldwin's colors no longer ornamented their breasts.

Four men sauntered out of a nearby alley, but they were not French. The French remembered San Nicolo and would have wished the lads well. These four wore Venetian colors, and they were looking for trouble. William and Tom kept up their steady pace but drew closer together.

A shout rose behind them. "Ha! Some of Montfort's men, who think themselves too good to help Venice! Let's give them a taste of what it means to oppose Venetians."

The cobblestones were drier than they were in the mornings, when slops came sloshing from the upper stories of the houses lining the street, but there were still wet spots. Tom chose the driest and stopped to face the oncoming quartet, William beside him.

"We are on an important errand and have no wish to delay," Tom stated quietly.

Gladly William let him speak. He would have hated to have his own voice quaver or break at such a time.

"I'll bet you have business elsewhere!" the leader of the group replied scornfully. "Out with your swords, or we will kick you like puppies down the street."

The boys had had plenty of practice with their weapons but had never unsheathed them in actual combat. Now they had no choice. William sidestepped a rush and swung his blade out. Tom already seemed entangled with two of the opponents. Their numbers handicapped them. A good thing that practice does pay, William thought as coolly as if he were outside the event, watching. He did not have to stop to remember what move came next.

"A Montfort!" Tom shouted. Good idea, that! Anyone hearing the clash of metal would know who was under attack.

The shutters of surrounding houses remained tightly closed, but both up and down the street came shouts of inquiry.

"A Montfort!" Tom barely had breath for the words. William had an instant of admiration for his squire, whose arm seemed untiring. The Venetians attacked harder, eager to overcome the unexpectedly skillful pair before help arrived.

To counter a savage downstroke at his head, William brought up his sword. But his assailant's weight allowed the Venetian to beat down the sword so that it hit the English lad's basinet with a sound like an anvil ringing, and glanced to slice his shoulder. He did not even feel the shoulder blow as he fell, his hand no longer holding the hilt of his weapon.

It lay beside him, and William reached for it clumsily with his left hand. Tom straddled him, his sword alive in the dim light. Vaguely William wondered how any human could move so fast. His wound didn't hurt, and he could not think why he lay on the cobbles when he ought to be helping Tom. He reached for the sword with his left hand because the right one did not work.

"A Montfort! A Montfort!"

From both directions came help. The Venetians tried once more to get through Tom's whirling blade. One yelped, dropped his weapon, and ran, holding his arm. Another collapsed flat on the ground. The other two fled.

Tom sank to his knees beside William, peering at him in the dim light.

"Willie! Willie!"

"Did you see that, Montfort!" Enguerrand shouted, unnecessarily because they were both close. "I never saw a better defense. I'll swear Young Tom would have finished it by himself. You know what he has earned, Simon! He is in the right position, and if you don't, I will!"

William looked past Tom's bent head to see Simon with drawn sword. That's strange, he thought. The Venetians were gone, except for that one dragging himself away into the shadows. He would get away if they didn't watch it.

No one seemed to notice. Simon's blade reached out to touch Tom's shoulder gently with the flat. "It is my right. I call you to witness," Montfort said. Then, "Rise, Sir Thomas."

Tom looked up, oblivious. "William is bleeding. I don't know how badly he is hurt. His eyes are open."

"Of course," William replied clearly. "Oh, Tom! What would your gran'ther say!"

"What?" Tom asked.

His young master felt too tired to answer. Let someone else tell Tom he had been knighted "on field of battle," as said in the romances. Dully the boy heard Enguerrand say, "I claim the honor of giving him the belt. I suppose you will insist on giving the spurs yourself, Montfort."

If they would just go away, William thought, I could go to sleep.

Two people picked him up to carry him, and the movement hurt.

"He is bleeding a lot," someone said.

William did not care.

When he roused, though, it was a different matter. Pain throbbed through him. His head still rang with the sound of the blows. His shoulder seemed on fire, and his side felt caved in.

"My side?" he asked aloud. "I thought it was my shoulder."

Tom ran quickly to him, his face not the sober mask people usually saw. It blazed with relief and gladness.

"I thought you never were going to wake up, William."

"I wish I hadn't. It was a mistake."

Tom held the basinet to show the deep dent in the top. "Think what would have happened if you had not worn it. Your shoulder wound is not deep, but it is in a bad spot. The armorer is weeping because the blade went through where he broadened the shoulder of your mail. Lord Montfort tries to convince him that such a blow must go through chain mail, but he cannot be consoled."

Careful not to jar the injured shoulder, Tom pressed gently on the side that ached so unbearably. "That," he announced, "is the print on your hide of your last gold bezants—purple splotches. The blow did not go through the chain mail there."

"Ugh. You wear the money belt, Tom. I have had it long enough."

The darker boy patted himself to show the belt's present location. Feet, armored and spurred, by the nature of the sound, clanked along the corridor outside the small room. Simon and Enguerrand stooped over William.

"Eh, boy, we're glad to see your eyes open," Montfort informed him.

William nodded carefully, afraid to intensify his enormous headache.

"We have a problem, William. Emeric of Hungary has an escort waiting for us on the mountain road. Thus we must leave soon lest we put them in more danger. We can send you to Venice on a ship, to meet us when we arrive there, or we can leave you here under Baldwin's care. He is willing to have you remain with him. The thing we cannot do is carry you with us. I'm sorry."

His tone allowed no room for argument.

"Peter will stay with us," Tom explained to his young lord. "Wulf also. He does not want to go to Constantinople. Therefore he will attach himself to us and either go to the Holy Land or return home later."

Montfort smiled at the question in William's eyes. "Yes, they are your men. I will let Baldwin know. He says you have earned any housing and supplies you need. Your troops will be quartered right here." He chuckled. "You have nothing to fear from the Zarans. You lads are heroes in their eyes, having bested some of their ancient enemies."

"I did not!" William protested. "It was Sir Thomas here."

As Tom scowled, Montfort grinned. "You wouldn't believe the trouble we had getting his belt and spurs on him. Practically had to hold him down by force." Then, with a laugh at Tom's angry red face, he qualified his statement. "Well, not quite that bad, but I never met a man who accepted knighthood with poorer grace."

Feeling his eyelids drooping, William clutched his friend's hand. "At least you had the vigil with Humphrey and repeated the vows with him."

"And I will keep them better than many knights we have seen lately," Tom promised.

Montfort put an arm around the new knight and bent to William. "I will somehow send word where you may meet us in the spring. God keep you, lads."

He clanked off. As William sank into a doze shot with pain, he dimly heard the commotion outside as the company rattled off down the now deserted cobblestone streets and passages.

The boy found it difficult to appreciate the care his "troops" gave him. They would not leave him alone to sink into a feverish stupor, but were always changing the bandages, always making him drink something, usually nasty. They paid no attention to his fretfulness.

Peter came in one day with a lighter step. "I talked to a knight Hospitaler at the quay. He said we must have him out of this room when the sun shines, and open the dressings so the sun shines in. They learned that from the Saracens! He says it works well on slow-healing wounds."

"I don't want to be moved," William objected, but no one seemed to hear him.

As Tom stayed by to chase flies, the sun eased the pain of the inflamed tissues. William's head stopped ringing, and the purple of his side changed to a handsome green and yellow. At the same time he grew curious about the Hospitalers.

"Everyone welcomes them," Tom enthusiastically told him, "because they take in and care for the wounded and sick of all nations. Their real name is Knights of St. John—named for two Johns, one who succored Jerusalem hundreds of years ago, and for St. John the Baptist. They had a hospital in Jerusalem until the Saracens drove them out. Now they have no settled home except a hospital in Rhodes. These particular ones are on a mission to Rome."

"And what do they think of *this* Crusade?"

The invalid frowned at the rain that kept him in his room.

"Their silence is very loud," Tom assured him. "May I bring one of them to see you? He's not the same one who told us of healing sunshine. But he's unhappy with the hospitality of those who spend their nights drinking and gambling—he really means his vows." At William's nod, Tom added, "Sir Reginald intended to join his brother knight, but storms prevented it. I will go for him."

## Chapter Eleven

The Hospitaler stood lean and dark in his black robe with the eight-pointed white cross on the left breast. The cross resembled four spearheads meeting point to point at the center, a pleasant change from the white cross of the trouble-plagued Crusade the two lads had pledged to assist.

The dark visage brightened into a smile as the healer came into the room. William heard the swish of chain mail under the robe. The man was not only a healer but also a knight. He cared for the sick, and also defended them when necessary. But the knightly order's reputation was so great that it was seldom necessary.

"Here is a young Crusader who could not wait for the Holy Land for wounds!" Tom stated.

"I did not really go out and pick a fight!" William protested.

The Hospitaler gave him such an understanding glance that the boy knew he had heard the story.

"Sir Thomas, may I look at the wound?"

Tom, although ready to object to his title, shut his lips tightly and removed the clean pad he had just put on. The knight pulled a candle closer and looked carefully at the inflamed and puffy edges, like bruised lips around the gash. He lifted the bandage for a sniff, his nostrils twitching as though he did not like what he smelled.

"Does pus well out of it at times?"

"Yes!" Tom exclaimed. "It has been more than a

month, and it will look like it's doing all right, then pours out awful greenish-yellow stuff."

"His shoulder was bruised deeply, as well as slashed. The deep injury must heal, then the upper layers. It is not good to have the skin heal, then burst open with corruption from below."

Almost limp with relief that a skilled one would advise him, Tom sat back. "I thought it must be very bad because it wouldn't heal over."

Although William felt like some object being discussed, he did not mind. He enjoyed watching the expressive eyes and face of the Hospitaler. Here he found someone so worth knowing that it was almost payment for the wounding. To think the man gave up all other honors to serve Christ this way, when he would have been an adornment to any court.

"Thank you, Sir Reginald," Tom said humbly. He too felt the true greatness of the knight.

"Brother Reginald," corrected the Hospitaler. "If I were not on official business and obedience-bound, I could take you to one of our hospitals, William. As it is, I must cross the Adriatic as soon as possible. You have not heard from Montfort?"

"No, and I worry about it," Tom confessed. "When the weather clears for spring, the Crusaders will sail for the Eastern empire, and we want none of that. To be stranded here after they leave will not be good, though the Zarans are kind. They could not protect us against the hostile Venetians."

The Hospitaler brooded, a foot on a stool and his elbow on his knee. "I will sail in April. It is now February. In six weeks I will be in Ravenna, across the Adriatic. Could you pay for transportation to that city? I will give you names of persons to reach there. Of course, this is only if Montfort does not summon you before then."

William hung onto the hand offered him, hoping his face did not betray too much of his relief. Tom threw a look of approval over his shoulder, at the boy's restraint, as he led the Hospitaler away.

"Thank You, Lord Jesus," William murmured. "Even when we are disappointed in those we thought we could trust, You still have noble men in Your service."

The damp days wore on. All William's other injuries had healed, but he had to be careful with his right arm lest the tissues pull apart as they closed. Wulf and Captain Peter entertained him with their stories and wranglings, and he did appreciate their efforts, although the stories were old now.

Then the ring of other steps and the sound of voices arguing amicably in the hall came most welcome one day. "Conan! Bless you for coming. I needed some sunshine on this gray day."

"Not only have you this little ray of light"—Conan stretched his muscular figure—"but I bring you Rambaud and Guy of Coucy. Could any invalid ask more?"

William grinned. "Only to ask you how it became so boring elsewhere that you take refuge here!"

Rambaud dug an elbow into Guy's ribs. "A bright one, this lad. Others grew so tired of our strumming that we came to practice here. Why?

Because you are too weak to throw us out!"

The boy shook his head. Who could possibly tire of these three, greatest of their trade?

Conan unslung his lute from his back and set about tuning it. "Would you hear our latest?"

After some hours Tom returned to find them still at it. William croaked a greeting. The troubadours had urged him to join them, and in spite of an occasional surprising change in his voice, he had enjoyed it, even the laughs at his breaks.

"Have you heard Abelard's lovely song?" Conan asked. The men were about to depart, but stopped for one last verse. "Especially for you," he said.

"Oh, what their joy and their glory must be,
   Those endless sabbaths the Blessed Ones see!
Crown for the valiant! To weary ones, rest.
God shall be all, and in all ever blessed."

It was farewell enough, and without further word the musicians left.

"A good day, William?" Tom inquired.

A deep sigh answered him. The wounded boy had exhausted himself with excitement, and for once nightfall found welcome.

Wulf and Captain Peter sat burnishing their weaponry and helmets so all would be ready in case they had to make a quick move.

"The horses are doing well?" William inquired.

"Hah!" Wulf said no more.

Peter jerked a thumb at him. "Yours was fresh enough that he went out from under yon grumpy one. You notice he sits carefully."

Tom, even more silent than usual, waited until the two had gone to bed before he presented his latest news. "Boniface has received some secret envoys from Rome. I stopped at Montferrat's headquarters and recognized them. They avoided the Venetians. Apparently the Holy Father will forgive the French for their sin of attacking Christians, but not those of Venice. They have never repented and asked pardon! I am sure the envoys are warning Montferrat against taking up Alexius' cause and going against Constantinople."

"Boniface has signed the agreement, as well as St. Pol, Louis of Blois, and Baldwin," William said. "All great lords. I don't see how they can withdraw. Their share of the loot here did not pay their debt to Venice. That two hundred thousand marks Alexius promised looks very tempting."

"Shall I begin to look for passage to Ravenna?" Tom asked. "There is some shipping other than that of Venice."

His young lord nodded. "We can leave before the French get too involved in their own sailing. Do we have enough bezants?"

"I could wish we had more." Tom felt his belt. "Baldwin has housed us here, but in Ravenna we do not know how we will fare."

William's smile brightened the patient face he had worn during the months of his illness. "I think we can trust Brother Reginald. He would not misdirect us."

Conan came again the next day, bringing a surprising gift. The bent-necked lute he placed in the boy's hands had been used until the wood of its belly and sides had been worn pale. Conan demonstrated how to tune the instrument, then struck a chord. "There! You can use your right hand well enough for this, even if you cannot raise your arm. When your voice settles, it will be a good one, and in the meantime, practice on this. It's yours."

"Mine?" William looked with unbelief at the graceful old instrument. He caressed it with trembling hand. "I never was allowed even to *touch* my sister's lute. Will I hurt it, from ignorance?"

His eyes lifted to Conan's laughing face.

The troubadour shook his head. "The instrument is not really holy! It's meant to be handled and enjoyed, a gift from the three of us, Rambaud, Guy, and me. We had a good time here with you."

Tom now felt no reluctance at leaving William alone. The English boy wore his fingers sore on the strings, only stopping because his squire teasingly told him blood was not good for the lute! His right arm grew stronger with the constant exercise, but only from the elbow down. He had to move the upper arm with his other hand.

Tom's racing feet threw him against the wall as he swung into the room. "A ship from Brindisi is unloading and will take on cargo for Venice, but will stop at Ravenna! They have space for the horses. Not much room for us, but it is only over one night, I hope, and the captain agrees."

With a grin William sat up, supporting his right elbow with the other hand. "We must tell Baldwin. But will he forbid us to leave?" His face grew anxious at the thought.

"I think we have good reason to go. Brother Reginald told us to meet him there if you needed him. If Baldwin sees your shoulder he will realize you need the Hospitaler! And he would not know how much it has actually improved. Oh, Willie! There is more chance of getting word of Simon over there!"

The great count of Flanders came himself to see his young English lieges. "Sir Thomas," he began, not understanding the boy's scowl at the title (he thought it unhappiness at the bared, gashed shoulder of his master), "this is very bad. I did not realize so much damage had been done or I'd have sent you back to Venice for care."

"The Hospitaler gave us instructions," Tom hastily interrupted, "and truly, my Lord, William is much better. But we still would like to see Brother Reginald again. He told us where to meet him in Ravenna."

"My poor lad!" Baldwin spoke kindly to the young invalid. "Of course you must go. You plan to take the Brindisi ship? I will have arrangements made for your passage. Here is a purse of bezants and denarii. Rejoin us if you can. I will always have a place for you."

The boys thanked him heartily and with some embarrassment. "He made up his own mind on the evidence," William assured his squire. He shivered. "I am glad I did not have his 'best medical care' in Venice."

The little ship had more comfortable quarters for them than had seemed possible until Baldwin took charge. The count's wishes carried much more weight with the captain than those of Tom, who had begun to look quite shabby.

Unlike Zara, independent Ravenna did not threaten the imperial ambitions of Venice. Her interests lay inland. Venice concentrated wholly on dominion of the sea.

On landing, William mounted his own horse, but to his disgust Tom did not allow him the reins. Old Peter held the horse's head in case it should be suddenly startled. Their gear occupied the backs of the other two horses. Tom searched for someone to direct them.

"Oh, yes. We well know this name," a local citizen said. "This way, young sirs. For a denarius I will take you to the inn."

It was not one of the great hostelries, which relieved Tom's mind, considering their uncertain future. The innkeeper, on hearing the name of Brother Reginald, welcomed them happily. He led them through the public part of the inn and through the kitchen. The door opened to a quite different scene.

"Here you are, my lords. This is the Hospitalers' chapel. Here, the sleeping cells. There, their kitchen. Make yourselves comfortable, and wait. Noble Sir Reginald will come here directly on reaching Ravenna. Here is all that is needed for your own men to serve you." He smiled merrily, his hands folded over his paunch.

William nodded in gratitude. "We will do well here. Is there stable room for our three horses?"

"Indeed. The brothers keep that, also." The innkeeper's round face grew sad. "The good brothers lost their hospital in Jerusalem, but they have many small footholds such as this, and they keep a hospital at Acre in Palestine, as well as the one in Rhodes. Rest you well, knights."

The man seemed to believe that William had been wounded fighting Saracens. The boy did not feel like explaining that his injury came from so-called Christian allies.

Tom assigned each member of their party a small cell, but they spent most of their time in the cheerful kitchen, where Wulf and Peter argued about food preparation or anything else that came to mind. The flames of the cooking place cheered William, and he entertained his men by his interminable practice on the lute.

"Do you tire of hearing me?" he asked once.

"It is like the wind blowing," Wulf replied. " One listens or one pays no attention."

Tom laughed. "That will take down your pride, William!"

The young knight now rarely stayed around the inn. He wandered the streets of Ravenna, listened to gossip at the inns and market places. "I hope to hear something of Montfort without being conspicuous by asking. People talk of Venice, Zara, the Crusaders, but so far nothing of Simon."

One evening hoofs rang on the cobbles of the street beside the inn. A few robust voices penetrated through the thick wooden door. Its great lock creaked to an immense iron key, and Brother Reginald entered with his helpers. Tom he greeted with a slap on the back, William more gently with a grip to the forearm.

The big kitchen seemed full with all the knight's people who built up the fire and went to work. Instead of an inn, a temporary place, it became a home.

## Chapter Twelve

Reginald also brought some news. "Montfort and his company bypassed Venice and are heading south by stages. Having sent a messenger to the Holy Father, he has the blessing of Innocent. He hopes to join the papal envoys who will be going to Acre. Do you wish to go with him to Palestine?"

A long silence followed. William looked up with a small smile. "I could be of no use there. When you have time to look at my shoulder, perhaps you will know, but I am sure I can never wield a sword again."

Without any change in his cheerful expression, Reginald nodded. "How about your men?"

William turned to them with a question in his face. Tom also glanced at Wulf and Peter.

Wulf cleared his throat. "I started on Crusade and I would reach the Holy Land, but I owe much to the young sirs and I will not go while they need me."

Peter agreed. "I have known Lord William since his first step, and the only way I will leave him is that he send me."

Reginald's smile lit up. "And how about Sir Thomas?" Tom's jaw squared. "I will not leave him even if he sends me!"

Now the Hospitaler laughed aloud. "I will dispatch a messenger to tell Montfort you are here. We will talk later. Good men! Many a lord could wish for such faithful followers."

William felt his face flush, and lowered his eyelids lest a teary shine show. *His* men!

Reginald taught him exercises for both his injured arm and the whole body. He started Tom on working the wasted upper portion of the arm, and in spite of William's yelps, the dark lad persisted.

"Now, Lord William, you practice the same skills on Sir Thomas."

"No!" Tom protested.

In spite of his objections, William pounced on him. Tom's hard muscles were a different matter from the soft ones of his ailing lord, but the blond boy learned every skill Reginald taught them. The exercise, as well as the massage, strengthened him until he could even walk out to see parts of the city.

William and his men wore chain mail under their outer garments. His drooping shoulder made alterations necessary to all his clothing, including the mail. However, they could never entirely remove the dent from his basinet. It would be a reminder that the helmet had saved his life. Peter briskly polished it anew.

"An honorable scar. You would not wish it forgotten."

"It is not likely that I will forget!" The lad answered wryly.

To Ravenna the envoys of the pope now came with pomp and ceremony rather than secretly. They had arranged for ships to convey a large number to Acre in Palestine. Enough Crusaders had left the lords at Zara, or had never joined them, to make a respectable army.

William's enthusiasm for crusading had somehow vanished.

"No pains in your stomach over it?" Tom teased.

"No," William answered placidly. "I am getting a new vision."

The dark boy gave him an interested stare, but his friend and lord said no more.

The lute and its player became popular for evenings lit by the remnants of the cooking fire. William needed no light to tune his instrument or finger it. Reginald's helpers loved most the sacred songs of older times, as well as the new Crusader ones. More and more William dwelt on these peaceable words:

"O Jesus, ever with us stay,
   Make all our moments calm and bright.
 Chase the dark night of sin away,
   Shed o'er the world Thy holy light."

A favorite composer, Bernard of Clairvaux, resting in Jesus now for fifty years, drew him over and over.

"What language shall I borrow
   To thank Thee, dearest Friend,
 For this Thy dying sorrow,
   Thy pity without end?

"O make me Thine forever;
   And should I fainting be,
 Lord, let me never, never
   Outlive my love to Thee."

News arrived that the Venetian fleet prepared to sail for Constantinople. The French and their allies from Zara had joined it. The quiet life in the hospice of the Hospitalers grew just a little dull, but the boys could not plan anything until Montfort came.

Would he ever show up?

William trudged along, hardly seeing the cobbles beneath his feet, the street vendors, or the overhead balconies that darkened the way. Tom sauntered a little to the rear, watchful for signs of tiredness in his young lord. A knight rode imperiously through the crowd, scattering people to each side as they tried to avoid being trampled. With a frown William watched. Tom pulled the blond boy back.

"Note the beard and the red cross? Who only wears that combination?"

His lord's frown did not lessen. "Templars. The rival organization to the Hospitalers."

Tom nodded. "With the same vows of poverty, chastity, and obedience. Note his rich horse trappings and cloak. Not just silver on the bridle, but gold! No wonder Brother Reginald shakes his head with that odd little smile when we ask about the Knights of the Temple."

"See how arrogantly he drives people out of his way. I cannot imagine Reginald doing the like."

The two paused to watch the further progress of the knight. Tom caught a quick breath as an iron hand clamped on his shoulder. William looked up and with a choking cry flung himself at the fist's owner.

"Simon! How you surprised us!" Forgetful of dignity, the English lad embraced his patron with his good arm. Then, suddenly embarrassed, he stood back and tried to apologize.

Montfort grinned and shook his head. "You were so involved in admiring yon peacock you could not see anything else."

"I would not say *admi*re is the exact word." Tom's face puckered a little.

The baron shook his head more seriously. "The Templars are getting more powerful and more corrupt every day. It behooves youngsters like you to stay out of their way."

William agreed. "Brother Reginald says pride is a great danger to any order. He is thankful that the grand masters of the Knights of St. John, the Hospitalers, are set on keeping simplicity and the original vows."

"That is the man I want to see. Take me to Brother Reginald. I will thank him for his help to you."

The boys were pleased to bring Simon to their home of the past weeks. They need not be ashamed of the Hospitaler and his assistants.

"I am most happy with the way this lad looks." Simon squeezed William's left arm while he talked to their host. "Some of my men doubted that he could live, even without use of the arm. Richard of England and Normandy died of a lesser wound."

"He had excellent helpers, who cared for him whether he would or not!" Reginald replied. "You can see that he has good use of the forearm and hand, and is stronger every day. He has new and useful accomplishments, too."

"I will never bear sword in that hand again, sir."

He did not appear visibly depressed over the prospect.

"In any case," Reginald reminded them, "I wish to keep him under my care for some time yet. May I take William and Sir Thomas on to Rhodes, where I am assigned to our new base and hospital? It is much nearer the Holy Land, with constant shipping going in all directions. When he is fit for duty I will send you word. However, in my galley there will be no room for horses or William's other two men."

A throat cleared behind them. "Wulf and I with the horses could go with Lord Simon if he permits," Peter said.

"If he permits!" Montfort laughed. "You old fraud! You know I'm desperate for old campaigners who can whip a rabble into an army. The horses too are welcome."

William grinned without regret. "Then the horses Lady Alix gave us will get there even if we do not."

Montfort found the papal envoys, and they accepted him gladly, making space in their ship for his extensive company.

Peter could hardly speak for grief at leaving the English lad. "If it were not for Sir Reginald, I would not go," he growled.

Wulf snorted. "The Hospitaler can do more for him than you can."

The English captain nodded jerkily. "We will meet again, somewhere."

"At Rhodes," Brother Reginald cheerfully informed him.

William wondered about that. "But they start

much before us," he said.

The Hospitaler did not explain the twinkle in his eyes. The boys would learn. The Knights of St. John had a unique system of transportation. Their galleys, as much as one hundred feet long but only six feet wide, could travel exceedingly fast, though they never used them in storms except in saving lives.

"You see no slaves," Reginald indicated when they had boarded one. The men at the sweeps were all brawny brother-sergeants with the eight-pointed white cross on their breast. "I, too, will take my turn at the rowing bench. We carry no dead weight other than the ill or wounded."

Tom's eyes sparkled, and he flexed his arms, making William laugh. "I have one good arm too!" he said.

"You will be more lopsided than ever," Tom countered, "if you develop rowing muscles in that."

"Ha!" William retorted. "We will see if a Bohun with one good arm isn't the equal of a Dobbins with two!"

Reginald seemed concerned for a moment until he realized that they were only continuing a friendly controversy. "I do notice that William will be a big man when he gets his growth," he said.

Tom swaggered as he walked away. "Bigger but never better. My gran'ther would skin me if I didn't stay ahead if only by so much!" And he measured with his thumb and forefinger.

Little baggage went with them. "We have hospices at most major harbors, with all we need in store," Reginald explained. "We dare not overload the galley, for we never know when we may pick up those in need of care."

So Tom took a place at the sweeps, determined to show that a Wye man could outrow anyone else. William sat in the stern behind the man who beat the time.

The long galley slipped gently and easily between other craft, the men at the long oars not seeing where they went, but watching intently the motions of their leader. Tom caught on fast after disrupting the rhythm a few times when the hand motions of the coxswain confused him.

After they were clear of the congested harbor, the sweeps' timing picked up until they skimmed over the water so lightly it was hard to believe. They sat low in the water, altogether different from the high deck of a sailing ship. William found himself swaying in time to the rhythm and made himself lie back and relax. He would work later.

## Chapter Thirteen

*T*he narrow, speedy vessel fled over the sea like a many-legged water insect. The water dimpled along side as the long oars dipped and raised. Tom's jaw set grimly as he kept the beat. He could not see the grins on the faces of his fellow oarsmen as the tempo increased again and again. Finally Reginald raised a hand and cried, "Enough!"

The sweeps lifted and folded neatly against the sides of the vessel. Then Tom heard the laughter and turned to face the others. "Well done, lad! Well done!" they shouted.

" You have proven Wye men to our satisfaction. We seldom find a recruit who can keep that pace."

The galley coasted. "Now let us see what this other Wye man can do," the "timekeeper" suggested.

"Not as well as Tom," William murmured as the boys changed places.

He watched the coxswain's cues and with care missed being thumped in the back by the sweep behind him. Concentrating wholly on his job, he dared not even glance at Tom's dark face agrin. Pull! Straighten legs against the footboard, leaning back with the heave, then down, lifting the heavy, wet weight above the water. Thrust forward, bending low. Let the blade dip deep into the sea, then pull. Again. Again.

With only one hand to use, though it had strengthened and broadened with use, he grew quickly short of breath, but would not call for mercy. Brother Reginald watched closely to note the whiteness about the boy's mouth and the drops of sweat trickling down.

"Hold!" he called. "Now it is my turn."

The smiles died away among the oarsmen, and they settled themselves more firmly. It seemed that Reginald would provide more of a contest with the other oarsmen.

The boys' eyes widened at the speed the light galley now attained. Ahead of them a cargo ship labored, sails spread, but it seemed to stand still or even to slip backward to meet them. Its ungainly cargo made a greater contrast between the sleek speedster and the lumbering ship.

"A Venetian," Tom spoke in William's ear. "Those are siege machines. It goes to join the rest of the fleet at the island of Corfu. See the sailors stare at us. They wonder what mission the Hospitalers forward with such haste."

That night at another hospice, Reginald commented on the mighty fleet gathering against Constantinople. "I doubt that they will need so much. The emperor is so in love with his pleasures that he has done nothing about defenses beyond the wall and its towers. The only soldiers are mercenaries hired by the empire. No Byzantine citizens have learned the arts of defense."

"But their fleet!" William protested. "I have heard that their navy numbers sixteen hundred vessels."

"None of which have anchors, masts, or sails! The admiral of the navy has even sold all the nails that could be drawn out for his own profit. There are not more than twenty worm-eaten hulks to defend the city."

"Have their spies not given them warning of this attack?" Tom asked.

"Of course. But the emperor refuses to allow any timber cut from the few forests left. They are his game preserves. Thus the navy has nothing to build or repair vessels."

The stunned boys stared at him. "They almost deserve to be conquered," Tom said indignantly.

Reginald nodded. "I agree. But not by Christian knights sworn to save Jerusalem from the Saracens."

William's head drooped. "It makes me feel bad that men I admired, such as Conan of Béthune and Count Baldwin, should have part in this."

"Venice is skilled at making her wishes sound like right. Also Constantinople is the richest city in the world. Even such honest men as Conan and Baldwin may be tempted by the wish to at least see it. The pathetic story of young Alexius appeals to chivalrous hearts. However, his claim to the throne rests on poor reasons. His father had no more right to it than the uncle who stole it."

William gave Reginald a twisted smile. "I started on this Crusade with such high and holy hopes. Now I have seen so much cheating and self-seeking in it that it has soured the whole thing. What of the tens of thousands who died trying to cross the Alps? Did they waste their lives for nothing?"

"Oh, lad!" Reginald answered him. "Remember, our Lord still has His faithful ones. Whether Jerusalem below is ever freed we cannot know now, but we can know that Jerusalem above will open her pearly gates for His blessed ones when the time comes. Many who perished in the Alps died in faith and hope and will see the better Jerusalem. Do not despair. We still have a work to do for Christ, whatever disappointments may haunt our ways!"

The lad looked as though he still wished to say something, but was uncertain how the Hospitaler would receive it. Tom spoke for him. "We like your kind of work for our Lord. It is building up instead of destroying. There must be great satisfaction in giving oneself to it."

Reginald's thoughtful expression lightened. "You are right. I would prefer my state of mind to that of Baldwin any day! However, there are risks here, as well. Men seek power, and power feeds on itself. Each of us must keep his close link to our Saviour and let nothing separate us from God."

The brother-helpers had cleared the table, and the room grew quieter as William's words sounded clearly. "How does one become a Knight of St. John?"

The Hospitaler considered him. "There are three ranks among us: knights, who must belong to noble families, brother-priests, and brother-sergeants or -helpers. Each is sworn to absolute obedience. Also, to poverty, with nothing of his own. We may serve our noble patients on silver plates, but we eat from ordinary pottery. To chastity, keeping ourselves clean for Christ. To service to the many of this earth who desperately need help, whether sick, wounded, or poor. We began in Jerusalem tending those injured trying to keep the Holy City from the paynim.* But our work has broadened since losing our great hospital there, so perhaps the loss has had some good results.

"Each country has a motherhouse that accepts and trains applicants no younger than 14 years. At 18 they may become full Knights of St. John and may be sent anywhere to serve."

Tom looked gloomy. "I could become a brother-helper."

William laughed. "Now, Sir Thomas! You are already a knight!"

The dark boy hit the table with his fist, making its solid bulk tremble. "I am Tom Dobbins! I will not accept anything that is not the proper due of Tom Dobbins!"

In mock humility his young lord bent his head. "As you wish. What worries me is that I am only 13. I cannot apply for months yet."

Brother Reginald chuckled. "Which gives you time to consider whether it is your true calling. Part of the time you will spend at Rhodes, learning. Part of it will pass on the seas or possibly crossing France to get home. Also, you will spend some of the time visiting your family. They may not wish you to become a Hospitaler."

William grinned, but not in amusement. "I doubt that King John will insist on my presence at court. There are troubadours in plenty to sing lovesick tunes to the ladies, and I prefer other songs." He reached for his lute and idly fingered

---
*paynim: non-Christian, Moslem

chords as they talked.

"Lads," Reginald confessed, "you must know that I have in mind the order of the Knights of St. John for you both. That is the reason for bringing you with me. William could have recovered with Simon of Montfort, though possibly not as fast or with such strength. However, you have time to think it over and see more of our work before the final decision. Here, let me give you these as a symbol of our interest in you."

He produced a pin for each to wear on the breast, where the eight-pointed star adorned him. Each pin had a miniature of that cross in white enamel on gold.

"To make you welcome at any of our hospices. The pins always remain the property of the order, however. When you have the right to wear the badge of full membership or when you decide against it you must return them"

William looked down at his pin with a surge of joy greater even than at receiving the white cross of the Crusade. His fingers struck sure notes.

"This song is my prayer for us and for all the true and faithful who are captives in a world of greed and suffering."

> "O come, O come, Immanuel,
>   And ransom captive Israel
> That mourns in lowly exile here
>   Until the Son of God appear.
> Rejoice! Rejoice! Immanuel
>   Shall come to thee, O Israel!"

# Epilogue

The Venetians and French took little time to capture the great city of Constantinople, for the usurper uncle fled with a favorite daughter and all the gold he could carry, leaving the rest of his family to captivity. The victors crowned young Alexius coemperor with his blind father, whom they had rescued from a dungeon.

However, the Greeks hated Alexius and refused to pay the Crusaders what he had promised. Even by melting down silver vessels from the churches he could not come up with the sum. Of course, robbing the churches enraged his subjects even more.

The conquering force had camped outside the city, but now they moved in, fighting more among themselves than with the Greeks. They looted and almost destroyed the city. The Crusaders melted down many great works of art and ancient sculptures to coin money. One work of art salvaged was the group of four horses that now adorns St. Mark's in Venice. The clergy were so busy collecting relics and teasures in competition with one another that they had no control over the looters.

The Knights of St. John (Hospitalers) grew greater and more renowned for centuries. Worldliness crept in, as so much power invites, but their reputation never grew as bad as that of the Templars.

Baldwin of Flanders became emperor of Constantinople, but the Latin kingdom existed only for fifty-seven years before the Greeks regained it. Eventually the city fell to the Moslems, who still hold it, calling the city Istanbul.

Both Earl Henry and Young Humphrey joined the other barons of England in forcing King John to sign the Magna Charta about ten years after the events of this story. That great document is the foundation of English freedom, though the barons really had their own welfare in mind rather than that of common people.

Henry de Bohun took the cross fifteen years after the Crusade of the white cross, and died on Crusade. He left Humphrey to become warden of the Welsh Marches, constable of England, earl of Hereford and Essex. The family remained prominent in English history for generations. A great-grandson, also named Humphrey, married Princess Elizabeth, daughter of Edward I of England.

It is hard to believe that our Saviour instigated the frenzy of the Crusades. Greed for name, fame, power, or wealth spoiled every one. The enormous numbers who perished on Crusade, even multitudes of children, we may safely leave to God's judgment.

# Bibliography

Archer, T. A., and C. L. Kingsford. *The Crusades, Story of the Latin Kingdom of Jerusalem.* New York: G. P. Putnam's Sons.

Archer, T. A. (ed.). *The Crusade of Richard I, 1189-1192.* New York: G. P. Putnam's Sons, 1889.

*Atlas of Early Christian World.* Nelson, 1959.

Blackwell, Basil. *Who's Who in History,* Vol. I. Oxford, 1960.

Brandel, Fernan. *The Mediterranean and the Mediterranean World of Philip II.* Harper & Row, 1970.

Dicks, T. R. Brian. *Rhodes.* Harrisburg, Pa.: Stackpole Books, 1974.

Duggan, Alfred. *History of Knights of Malta.* New York: Pantheon Books, Inc., 1963.

*Encyclopedia of World Art.* Art., "Costumes." 15 vols. New York: McGraw-Hill Book Co., 1959-1968.

Feist, Aubrey. *The Lion of St. Mark.* Indianapolis: Bobbs-Merrill Co., Inc., 1971.

Funck-Brentano, Frantz. *The Middle Ages: National History of France.* Bretane, 1922.

Gardner, John C. *Life and Times of Chaucer.* Introduction. Westminster, Md.: Alfred A. Knopf, *Inc.,* 1977.

Kelly, A. R. *Eleanor of Aquitaine and the Four Kings.* Cambridge, Mass.: Harvard University Press, 1950.

Lane, Frederic C. *Venice: A Maritime Republic.*

Baltimore: Johns Hopkins Press, 1973.

*Latin Christianity*, Book IV.

Pernoud, Régine (ed. Trans. by Enid McLeod) *The Crusades*. New York: G. P. Putnam's Sons, 1963.

*Pilgrim Hymnal*. Pilgrim Press, 1931.

Ridpath, John C. *Ridpath's History of the World*, Vol. IV. 9 vols. Cincinnati: Jones Brothers Pub. Co., 1894.

Riviene-Sestier. *Venice and the Islands*. New York: G. P. Putnam's Sons, 1963.

Seton, Kenneth M. *A History of the Crusades*, Vol. II. University of Pennsylvania, 1962.

Strickland, Agnes. *Lives of the Queens of England*, vol. 2. Lea and Blanchard, 1848.

Treece, Henry. *The Crusades*. New York: Random House, Inc., 1963.

Williams, Henry. *Historian's History of the World*, Vol. XI.

*The World Book Atlas.* "The Crusades," Chicago: Field Enterprises Educational Corp., 1973. p. 47.

Some of the crusader hymns in the story are found in the SDA *Hymnal*, the others in the *Pilgrim Hymnal*.